By Donald Windham

Emblems of Conduct

But only to build memories of spiritual gates.

Emblems of Conduct

Donald Windham

Brown Thrasher Books

The University of Georgia Press

Athens and London

Published in 1996 as a Brown Thrasher Book
by the University of Georgia Press, Athens, Georgia 30602
© 1963, 1991 by Donald Windham
Chapters 2, 4, 7, 11, 12, and 16, in slightly different form, were first published
in *The New Yorker.* © 1960, 1962, 1963 by Donald Windham.

The paper in this book meets the guidelines for permanence and durability
of the Committee on Production Guidelines for Book Longevity
of the Council on Library Resources.

Printed in the United States of America
oo 99 98 97 96 P 5 4 3 2 1

Library of Congress Cataloging in Publication Data
Windham, Donald.
Emblems of conduct / Donald Windham.
p. cm.
Originally published: New York : Scribner's, © 1963.
"Brown thrasher books."
ISBN 0-8203-1841-8 (pbk. : alk. paper)
1. Windham, Donald—Biography. 2. Novelists, American—20th
century—Biography. 3. Atlanta (Ga.)—Biography. I. Title.
PS3573.I52467 1996
813'.54—dc20
[B]   95-26346

British Library Cataloging in Publication Data available

To Sandy Campbell

Above all, do not write your autobiography, for your childhood is literally the whole of your capital.

W. H. AUDEN

Contents

The Dark Night

What do I see when I am not thinking of anything and not looking at the sight in front of my eyes?

A green wooden house, three stories high, in Atlanta, Georgia, on Peachtree Street, between Twelfth and Thirteenth. Thirteenth Street does not cross Peachtree. If it did, it would go through the side yard, taking off a part of the long front porch. Eight square Ionic columns, one story high, support the porch roof across the face of the house, and others go back on either side. Balusters, shaped like those on the terrace at Versailles, join the columns, their railings curving gracefully up at the side of each.

Above the ground floor, the house goes berserk. In the space over the front door, set back behind the slate roof of the lower porch, a second story loggia is enclosed with wooden spindles, curved like the arches of light bulbs in an Italian street fair. On the top story, similar arches fence in the four veranda openings of a corner tower. Around the angle of the building, in side porches and loggias, smaller versions of the Ionic columns pop up here and there, and at one point two full circles of the spindles, set close together, glare down at you like the eyes of an enormous owl.

The house boasts fourteen large rooms, their walls dark green or dark red, and various corridors, pantries, closets, baths, as well as the third story, undivided and unused, but with its full share of eccentric verandas. The rooms are full of heavy furniture, yet despite the furniture, there is space, day and night, summer and winter, inside and out. The property runs the depth of the block, from Peachtree Street to Crescent Avenue, and it is wide enough to contain another house of equal size. On the right, as you face it, in the place where Thirteenth Street would run, there is the old orchard and pasture, now known as the vacant lot. A long way back of the house there is the garage, a long way back of the garage, the barn, and back of the barn, a garden of dry corn stalks.

The house is unusual in two ways. It is bigger than the houses around it, even those that are its superiors in style and value. And it is made of wood. The other large homes are of brick, stone, and terra cotta. It is deliberately and defiantly of wood. It dares to be vulnerable in a way the other structures do not. It is as intent on permanence and solidity as they are, but it is willing, as they are not, to risk the elegance of oak and cedar, to turn its back on the business-tainted materials that stores and offices are built of. When it was erected, the memory of the Civil War, of the burning of Atlanta, and of the commercial reconstruction of the city in bricks, was not yet forgotten; it stands as an emblem of the new, proud, and never-to-end, grace and prosperity.

The winter night descended early. It was cold. Most of my grandparents' large old house was dark.

On one side of the downstairs hall, the lights were lit in the living room, where Mother was reading a chapter of the Bible to my brother and me.

On the other, in the parlor, Aunt Berta was sewing and her daughter was practicing the piano.

Lily Mae, the Negro cook, had gone home for the night, leaving the back of the house empty.

Beneath the moonless sky along Peachtree Street, the lamps shone on the bare branches of the trees whose green leaves caught their light in the summertime. Each of the frosted glass globes was painted opaque on the side toward the houses, leaving the winter front yards in darkness.

In the stretch of earth between the sidewalk and the stone curb, opposite the end of our front walk, a marble mounting stone with the name DONALDSON carved on it, shone like a one-hundred pound cake of ice. The nearest warm light was up the block on the other side of the street where the Albert Ice Cream Parlor was open, and beyond it on the bright vacant cement of the Gulf filling station at the corner, where the attendant was inside by the stove.

Our nearest neighbors were away. Across the wide vacant lot on the other side, in a red brick building, the McCrareys lived and maintained a photographic studio. A triptych-shaped

display cabinet in front of their house contained three photographs of girls in ankle length dresses, bouquets of roses in
their laps. But the display's single light bulb gave little il-
lumination. The McCrareys' front yard was almost as dark as
the back, where a morgue-like building, storing thousands of
photographic plates, stood opposite our unused barn, in which
a tramp recently had been caught sleeping.

Suddenly, a bang, like a pistol shot, sounded on our front
porch. Mother stopped reading. Across the hall, the piano
music ceased.

The front and back doors of the house were left unlocked
until the last person went to bed. My mother and aunt, despite
some irrational fears, were not afraid of housebreakers. While
they lived here where they had been brought up, they believed
that no harm could come to them, especially so long as no
outsiders were present. They probably felt even more secure
without their husbands, one dead, one divorced, than they
would have with them.

Mother and Aunt Berta had disagreed at the supper table
and were not speaking. Nevertheless, in a moment we heard
Aunt Berta leave the parlor. The door of the living room
opened and she asked:

"Did you hear anything?"

"Yes," Mother answered. "It sounded like a pistol shot."

"It sounded to me," said Aunt Berta, "like someone jumping
over the banisters onto the front porch."

Uneasily, Mother wanted to know if her sister had put the
night latch on the front door.

"Yes, and I'd better go and lock the back."

Aunt Berta went out, closing the door behind her. We heard her at the foot of the stairs, calling her son. He was the man of the house, and fourteen years old.

Mother went out into the hall to see what was happening. They were standing at the back end of the long hall, at the door of the closet under the staircase. In her hand, my aunt held the flashlight that was kept there to use when a scuttle of coal was brought in at night from the coal bin, outside the house and beneath the kitchen.

My cousin wanted to go out with the flashlight, but his mother said:

"If it's a burglar, Carl, he's probably still out there and he'll attack you. You can look through the windows just as well."

First, my cousin looked out of the parlor windows, shining the beam of the flashlight across the dark space between the walls of the house and the heavy columns and balustrade of the covered front porch. After the parlor, they went into the library. Then they came across the hall into the living room. Here a circle of windows, the base of the tower, opened onto the porch, and we all looked. But all that appeared in the beam of light was the dark banisters and columns, the yard, the driveway, and the hedge.

"What about the door to your room?" Aunt Berta asked.

"It's locked," Mother said, looking toward the next room, in which she slept and from which a door opened directly onto the end of the porch. "No one could get in, unless he forced the lock."

We stood, hesitating before the closed bedroom door. Then, from the other side of the house, the same bang was repeated. This time, it sounded to all of us like someone jumping over the banisters onto the porch. The frightened looks that this second explosion caused on my mother's and aunt's faces filled me with the kind of fear that makes the hair stand up on the back of your neck. For a moment, the living room was as cold as the unheated hall.

"I'm going to call Tommy," my aunt said.

While she went to the telephone, behind the portieres in the hall, Mother held the living room door open so her sister would not be alone.

My uncle, who lived only a block away on Thirteenth Street, arrived in a few minutes. When he had been told what had happened, he said:

"Well, whoever it was must be gone by now."

"Tommy, if he stayed here after we started looking for him, he won't have left now," Aunt Berta said. "Louise and I aren't ordinarily afraid to stay here alone. But whoever that was is in this house or waiting outside to get in as soon as we go to sleep."

"All right. I'll have a look around."

"Did you bring a gun?"

"One of my hunting rifles is upstairs."

Aunt Berta's daughter stayed with us while her mother and brother went upstairs with my uncle. They went through each of the six bedrooms with the flashlight, and out onto the two second story porches, from which they directed the beam of light onto the slate roof. They did not find a trace of anyone's having been there. Downstairs, they proceeded through the hall to the rear of the house. After searching the kitchen and the storage room behind it, my uncle, carrying his rifle, went outside.

"At least there's no one in the house," Mother said.

But I doubt that she forgot the attic, any more than I did. And although my uncle was searching the yard, what of the wide field of the vacant lot, with the pits at the back end where clay had been dug years ago for the manufacture of bricks? What of the narrow space beneath the house, into which my brother and I sometimes crawled? What of the stone wall where the level of the property dropped, and what of the posts of the driveway gate, which we hid behind when playing hide and seek, without being found even in the daytime? What of the second story of the barn, where the tramp had been, and what of the woodpile and the shapeless undergrowth of kudzu vines behind it?

It was far from a relief when my uncle came back without having found anyone.

"I don't think you ought to go home," Aunt Berta said. "Call Margaret and tell her we want you to stay the night here."

One of my main sensations of childhood is of being abandoned in a large house at night, a house that is empty, although our house never was, a house that someone is trying to break into. The rooms are bare, the furniture is gone, except for gold-framed photographs on the dark green walls, a pair of red portieres separating one section of the empty hall from the other. Outside, the wind brings its different noises. Around each corner, lies the unknown. But all that I ever see is empty floorboards and bare walls. The hand that rattles the window, the foot that creaks the step, vanish the moment my eye turns. This sensation reflects more than one dream, but all of the dreams recall that night as I lie trying to go to sleep. The fear I feel is the fear that has no known cause, the fear that dives down with you at the point where you doze to escape it, swims underwater in your dreams, and comes up again at the point where you awake. When I open my eyes, the neck of my pajama jacket is wet with sweat, and it takes a long time for me to be sure that the furniture is really there in the dark, my brother in the bed at my side, my mother in the next room.

In the morning, my uncle looks around the house again but finds no footprints or signs of anyone's having been there, and goes home, laughing at his sisters' fears.

Then, in the afternoon, we discover what has frightened us. It is the house itself. On the porch floor, almost beneath the swing, we discover two rectangles of the parquetry porch ceiling that have fallen the night before. Since my grandparents' deaths, no repairs have been made on their house, and the neglect is beginning to tell in the same way neglect is beginning to tell in the management of the money they left. But we are only relieved. We laugh at ourselves and at what has happened, and then forget these fateful, misinterpreted, and long to be ignored, sounds of warning.

The Man Who Could Not Come
Into the House

I have no memory whatever of the first six years of my life, when my mother, my brother, and I lived with my father. Consequently, I can picture my father as well in the period before I was born as when we were living with him; my awareness of his appearance at both times is from photographs. In the early pictures he is handsome, especially in the snapshot taken in front of the Sidney Lanier memorial in Piedmont Park, the summer he and Mother were married. The United States had entered World War I three months before, and the other men in the picture are in uniform. My father is in civilian clothes—a dapper white suit, a striped shirt, a bow tie. His straw hat is in his hand; his thick brown hair, combed up, flows back from his forehead in curling waves. His smile, beaming from lips and eyes, gives no hint that he had been discharged from the Army the previous year for his health. And there was very little wrong with him; he would have been subject to redraft that autumn, but by then Mother was pregnant with my brother, and married men with children were being deferred.

He looks more serious in the photograph taken two years later, in the fall of 1919, when mother was pregnant with me. He is dressed in a dark overcoat with a black velvet collar and is not smiling; but his expression of responsibility seems almost acted, as though it is an effort for him to prevent a smile from meeting the eye of the camera. His jaw is square, his lips are full, his eye almost disconcertingly direct—the responsible father of a family; but this, too, almost seems a self-dramatized pose rather than reality. The picture was taken in Philadelphia, where he had gone to work for the Disabled American Veterans. While he was there, he and my brother caught Spanish influenza; my brother developed double pneumonia; and Mother, nursing both of them, came down with influenza, too, and almost died.

The events also of this period I can picture as well as I can picture the early events of my life; my awareness of both is from having been told about them. In the spring, Father gave up his job and returned to Atlanta. Money was short, and he and Mother moved in with her sister, Aunt Ada, and her husband, in a small shingle house on Twelfth Street, a block away from the homeplace, my grandparents' house.

Aunt Berta was visiting them. On the first night of July, Mother's labor pains began, and when it was time for her to go to the hospital, Father's automobile would not start. He cranked the motor while Aunt Berta telephoned for a taxi and Aunt Ada held Mother's hand. The taxi was a long time in coming. The three women waited on the front porch. My father, in his shirtsleeves but wearing his tie and straw hat, like the hero in a James Montgomery Flagg illustration, remained at the curb alternately cranking and peering into the dark. When the taxi finally arrived, Aunt Berta and Father helped Mother onto the back seat. They had gone only a block when, as they turned into West Peachtree, the rear left tire went flat. The driver stopped and said that the tire would have to be changed; they must wait or get another taxi. But Mother was crying out as though I would be born any minute, and Father said that he would pay for the tire but that the driver had better keep going if he valued his life.

On they went, the flat tire flapping, the rim of the wheel cutting the rubber to shreds.

The doctor was at the hospital. He examined Mother, then went out to his automobile to fetch his case of instruments. A passing policeman, seeing him take them from the back seat, tried to arrest him as a thief. He escaped being carried to the police station by proving his identity, and the policeman said:

"Is that why that woman is screaming? I thought someone was being murdered."

It was a hot summer evening; the hospital windows were open to the street. Mother was weak from her illness, and her cries went on a long time. But fate did not wish to prevent my arrival, only to make it difficult; and, in the quiet hours of the morning, I was born.

It was not characteristic of my father to be present the day of my birth, and much of what I want to convey about him after that day must make its effect, as it did in my childhood, by omission. But he is present in the snapshots taken in Florida the next summer, when I was a year old, his salesman's smile beaming with an attraction that is irresistible; and it is easy to understand how he was a success in those days when the commodity of personality had not yet gone bankrupt. He had been the manager of the Hurt Building, in downtown Atlanta, when he and Mother married, but his true character was that of a salesman, and this is what he became now, selling insurance, automobiles, real estate. We lived in Orlando; he travelled all over the north of Florida and the south of Georgia. Money began to pour in, and although Mother never talked openly to me about him, she did say enough for me to know that it was when he was making money, rather than later when he was in financial trouble, that their marriage began to break up.

"There are some people, I guess," she said, "who cannot stand success and prosperity, and your daddy was one of them."

I must have been aware of the unpleasantness of these years to have forgotten them completely, but in all the photographs I myself appear as serenely happy as I remained for a long time to come—laughing on the sand at Daytona Beach, in front of our Stevens Salient Six touring car; smiling as I hold up a balloon at my brother's fourth birthday party in Tifton, where we lived for a while; frowning only in one photograph, in which I am standing in the sunshine on a cracked cement sidewalk, stark naked except for a sun hat. But beginning with the children's party photograph, after I have begun to walk, my father almost disappears from the album.

Everyone was making money in those years, and to him it must have seemed that his prosperity was only beginning: that with a little more luck, a little more indifference to those whose caution held him back, he could have everything he wanted. You have only to look into his eyes in the photographs to see that he was full of excitement and ambition—not ambition in the sense of desiring security but in desiring to project himself onto as much of the world as possible, and to absorb as much as possible of the world into himself. Security was what he had—money, a wife, children—and what else could a handsome and self-confident man do, surrounded by so much sensual bounty and multiplying money, except go further and further in pleasures and excitements and power? The answer, apparently, was that he could overextend himself and be hurt as much as he hurt those who tried to hold him back.

My father's brother, Hesper, lived in Florida at that time, and when Father began to disappear, first for days together, then for weeks, going to another city to escape the complicating alliances he had made, and writing to Mother to slip out of town and join him, Hesper was the only near person she thought of as a friend. She often used to tell me how nice he had been. Each time he came to the house, he brought a piece of candy or a stick of chewing gum to me and my brother. We would run to meet him, jump into his arms, kiss him, and ask where our presents were. And he, while we reached in his trouser pockets and searched for our gifts, would pretend to have forgotten or lost them. Then he liked to sit and hold us in his arms or on his lap; and I, for my part, was excessively full of affection and ready to give it to whoever would accept it. I have since been grateful that my father's parents had a son named after the evening star.

I thought that Mother left my father, and returned home to Atlanta without him, and I was surprised when I asked her and she told me that he came back with her. Drinking, neglecting his business, leaving town after town without paying his debts, and doing whatever else he did during those five years had had their effect; his money was gone by then. He returned with us and lived part of a year in the homeplace. But of his presence there, no matter how I search my mind, I can find no memory. The only hint of him I recall is a conversation between Mother and her oldest brother, in which she begged that she herself should not have to appear in court for her divorce, and that must have been a year after my father was gone.

Each summer we spent a month visiting my father's sister in the country, outside Columbus, Georgia. But Aunt Winnie had no more news of my father than we did. Only once, years later, did I hear her tell of his having turned up to visit her. He looked healthier than he had looked the last time she had seen him, and she thought that he had quit drinking. It turned out that he recently had been released from prison; in a fight in Florida he had knocked a man from a bridge into a river and the man had drowned. The conclusion the family drew from this was that he was a man who could behave well only in jail—but I, turning it around, saw my father as a man to whom propriety was a prison.

I do not know when I began romanticizing my father, but it is clear that I did it by the simple process of attributing to the person who was missing the qualities that were missing from the life around me. Mother had ample justification for the worst she thought of him. Among other things, after they were married she discovered that he had been married before, a fact that he had never given her a hint of. This was sufficient to prove even to her trustfulness that he was not as pure as his good looks or as straightforward as his smile. And it was natural, when he began to care for other things so much that he acted as though he never had cared for her, that she should think back to the year of their marriage, remember that unmarried he would have been subject to the draft again that autumn, and wonder how much this had had to do with his love for her.

After we returned to the homeplace, two of Mother's five brothers sometimes came to the house when they had been drinking, so I was aware of how unpleasant the worst characteristic my father was accused of could be. I was, in fact, often told that, with his absent warning and their present spectacle, I, surely, would never drink. And it would have been reasonable if I had attributed to my father the disagreeable traits I saw in them. But I did not. One difference cancelled everything: they had stayed at home and he had gone away alone. To them I attributed weakness and to him strength. And as a result, even later, when I realized that an unacceptable narrowness in their lives rather than an inherent taste for drunkenness caused their conduct, they remained the depository of all the coarse traits that must have been my father's as well as their own.

This quality of sticking close to home, which the family considered loyalty, appeared to me as weakness. My qualities, which the family considered sweetness, appeared to these uncles as weakness, too; and our rejection of each other was complete. Not at the beginning. If I had turned to Hesper with open arms, I turned to them even more eagerly when I no longer had even a part-time father. But to my uncles, with a surfeit of children and nephews, and with no paternal affection to spare but rather an excess of responsibilities and a need in themselves for more independence than they could find, my affection seemed effeminate and weak. And they lashed out at that weakness as though it were the thing in the world they most feared. When I was six they told me of a skeleton named Bloody Bones, who lived in the attic and came downstairs into the house at night. Then, when it was dark, they hid behind the portieres in the hall, jumped out, and grabbed me. No doubt I was supposed to overcome my fear and be rewarded with their respect and friendship, but my imagination gave an anthropomorphous character to the very dark itself. My reaction was to scream with terror. Their laughter gradually turned to epithets of disgust. I withdrew into myself, and with each encounter our mutual dislike increased. Whatever I did not know about my father, I knew he was in no way like these men.

He escaped, also, from being associated with the reprimands and restraints that inevitably fall upon one growing up. He never talked to me about the necessity of eating food I did not like, or told me that I should give up certain pleasures and do certain things because it was my duty to do them and that I would understand why when I grew up. I never associated him with the ridiculous warnings of sexual hygiene or with the worries about material security by which I was surrounded later. Most unfairly, I never associated him with those emotional difficulties that were specifically brought about by his absence.

There remain the two occasions on which I do remember having seen my father.

On the first I am not sure that I knew who he was. He came one day to the grammar school my brother and I attended. At noon recess he spoke to us in the gravel play yard; or rather, I think he spoke to my brother, who pointed me out to him as I sat on a bench near the wall, eating the sandwiches Mother prepared for us to take to school in brown paper bags; or, perhaps, even refused to point me out, for I think my brother believed we should have nothing to do with him, and I recall only a distant man towering at the edge of the yard full of small children.

But the other occasion I remember distinctly. It was early autumn, when the season is not certain and summer and autumn days are shuffled together like the red and black cards in a deck. Mother had spent the morning trying to decide whether or not to wash her hair. This depended on the weather, for when she had washed it and rinsed it in lemon-juice water, she sat out in the back yard, a white towel over her shoulders to protect her dress, and dried it in the sunshine. Her hair was auburn and unbobbed, and although she lamented that the sulphur in the water in Florida had darkened it, in the sunshine the highlights always gleamed.

It was Saturday. Aunt Berta and Lily Mae were cleaning the kitchen. Mother ought to be helping them. But if she waited until Monday to wash her hair, it might be raining again. Yesterday's drizzle had been brief, but sometimes this season of the year the rain lasted for a week. So, after helping Aunt Berta fill a wooden crate from the grocery store with trash and carry it out to the back yard to make a bonfire, she left us in the yard and went inside to wash her hair.

What a quantity of sticks there were in those days when everything was made out of wood. And how the wood blackened and crumbled. The front of the homeplace was kept more or less in good repair, but nothing in the back was ever mended. Where banisters had been knocked out, the space remained, gaping like the toothless gap in a mouth; the openings between the brick supports of the house, higher than in front, were partly covered by old boards, obviously used before for something else; and under the house could be seen the no-longer-used mahogany shutters from the front windows, stacked in the bare dirt, losing their finish.

My brother and I had made a town under one of the large oak trees. It consisted of stones collected from the yard and arranged along paths scratched in the dirt with the end of a broken banister. A stick (a slat from one of the blinds beneath the house), pushed along in the track that it itself had made, was a train going to and from other towns. We had played at this all morning. But it was after lunch and getting toward time for us to have our bath and go to the movies. And Mother had been inside a longer time than should have been necessary for her to wash her hair.

I went up the steps to look for her, but when I reached the porch, Aunt Berta, watching from the kitchen, told me to come in with her and wash my hands and face at the sink. My brother, too.

We protested. We were going to bathe soon. And I wanted to find Mother. Mother had a visitor, I was told, and we were to wash up and stay in the back. Aunt Berta was solemn and curt; in bewilderment, we obeyed her.

My brother was looking out the window, and I was sitting in the straight chair with the cowhide seat, helping the cook string beans, when Mother came back.

"Your daddy is here," she said, "and wants to see you."

He had not been allowed to come into the house. We were

led up the long hall and out onto the wide, square-columned and balustraded front porch.

He was facing the door, with his back to the yard and street. His hair was white, combed straight up and flowing back from his forehead in waves. His face was red. But he was not old; his hair had turned white by the time he was thirty, as mine was to, and his flaglike complexion was as much from living out of doors as from drink. He had brought my brother a fossil of a starfish, which he now gave to him, and while they talked I stood back and watched. Then, when he spoke to me, he squatted down with his elbows on his knees. My face was at the same level as his, and I looked into his blue eyes, large and filled with pink veins across the porcelain-like whites, repeating the colors of his hair and face. Mother stood behind us, waiting, but he spoke as though only the two of us were there.

He asked me if I knew that he loved me. Then he said that he did. And he told me not to forget it.

He was standing at his full height again. Aunt Berta, who had been waiting inside the door, led my brother and me into the house; and, through the living-room window, I watched him speak once more to Mother, turn, and go down the brick walk toward the passing traffic.

That was all.

His words to me on the porch had been ordinary, the ones called for by the occasion. But I was not reluctant to make the most of the commonplace. I accepted them unreservedly; and even if they were perfunctory, it made no difference. When you are given only one crumb, that crumb is gold.

Nevertheless, my acceptance was no climax. It had no more positive effect on my emotions than did my acceptance of the fact that the world is round. I did not treasure his words; I did not think of them. But my not *dis*believing them gave me that much more area of security, and of unawareness, to stand on. It created, I believe, one of the main differences between me and my brother, for to him the two years more of his memories must have made them sound hollow and false.

And, just as I did not think of his words, I did not think of my father. During the coming years, his figure did not enter the world I knew, any more than he had entered the house that day. The attachment to him of distant and romantic freedoms took place without my being aware of it. And even when I realized that I associated him with all those attractions that blossomed in flesh and flowers outside the house and yard I knew, it was not because my thoughts turned to him but because they turned to those attractions, and when I wondered why and what it was that I seemed to recognize in them, strangely enough it turned out to be the figure of my father, which I had created, unknowingly, and without any grounds, except the mutual absence of him and of them from my life.

His image, formed in the dark and under pressure, as diamonds are, became for me the more attractive half of the world.

What that half of the world became for him I discovered twenty years later, in a letter that should have wiped out at one stroke all the romance, but that, perversely, was perhaps the most romantic touch of all. He died in the Veterans Hospital in Bay Pines, Florida, from injuries received in fighting a forest fire. To my brother and me, as his legal heirs, was sent this list of all his worldly remains and possessions, to claim if we wished:

1 bathrobe
2 handkerchiefs
1 tube toothpaste, unopened
1 razor, safety
1 pocket hone
1 pair slippers
1 lot correspondence (no value)
a package of razor blades

```
*****************************************
        NOVEMBER SAVINGS

     Spend $50-$80, Save an extra
       10% off Purchase

   Spend $80 or more, Save an extra
       15% off Purchase

   Valid at Borders, 11/10-11/13/05

Barcode #:366007180000000000
POS: S3, S6, scan barcode, S2, 10/15%

Discount combines w/ all sale pricing
and in-store offers. Excludes gift
cards, periodicals, non-stock special
orders, shipping, online & previous
purchases. Discount on video games &
electronics is 10%. Cannot be used w/
any other coupons or standard group
discounts. Cash value .01 cent. Not
redeemable for cash. Any other use
constitutes fraud. One coupon per
customer, per day.
X                                      X
STORE: 0015    REG: 07/28   TRAN#: 8909
SALE           11/09/2005   EMP:  00186
*****************************************
```

Dr.
Jackson

1:30 ♀
Audiologue 2.00

12-1

993 Ferry
Refund
Sun J West
Suite 115
Bldg C
4 256.7532

The Bath Tub—I

◁◁◁From floor to ceiling, the spring air is fogged with
steam. I am sitting at the back of the tub, my legs spread
and one of my feet touching the white porcelain curves at
each side of my brother's buttocks. He is sitting in the middle
of the tub, directly in front of me. Somewhere in the water
the soap, which has sunk, is melting and filling the small
bathroom with an oceanlike fragrance; and my brother and I,
by moving our bodies back and forth, are creating a tide and
a slapping of waves. Near me, my washcloth rolls to the surface
like a sea-monster or a diving whale, then rolls down out of
sight again. I stop for a moment to see if it will reappear and
a wave, breaking against my body, sweeps over the back of
the tub and hits the wooden floor with a wet splash.

The bathrooms are on the second floor, with white marble
sinks and large mahogany-framed mirrors hanging above the
sinks; but the hot water tank downstairs supplies only enough
water for the ordinary uses of the kitchen; pots and kettles of

water have to be heated on the stove and carried up the long flight of stairs to the bathrooms on Saturdays when everyone bathes; and every Saturday, to lessen this task, my brother and I take a bath together.

I like my brother and I like doing things together with him. Most of my joy in this game of making a sea out of the bath water lies in the fact that it is his game and he is allowing me to join in it. My complete fondness for him is the earliest thing I can remember, and even before then, when I was just beginning to walk and talk, I am told, I used to break in half any cracker or cookie that was given me and wander about the house, searching for him and chanting:

"Give half to Freddie, give half to Freddie."

If I did not find him I would not give up. I would keep the half that was to be his and sing:

"Save 'til tomorrow, save 'til tomorrow."

Now that I am seven and he is nine there is no greater joy for me than that of joining my existence to his in experiences such as this one in the bath tub together. I am delighted for him to take charge and give orders so long as the orders make me a part of his activity. He began playing by floating a brush in the water, creating a current around the sides of the tub, and sailing the brush on it. He paddled forward with his left hand and backward with his right and directed me to do the same, keeping away from the back of the tub so the brush could sail completely around me and up to him again.

After that, holding on to the sides of the claw-footed tub and moving his body back and forth, he taught me to make waves. Then I stopped to look for the washcloth, the momentum of the water broke against my body, and—splash!—the wave went over the back of the tub.

Once before, when the two of us were playing some other game, water from the bathroom floor has seeped through and left a brown stain on the ceiling of the dining room below. We have been warned what will happen to us if this occurs again, and we lean over the back of the tub together and begin to sop up the water. But this does not work very well, especially as the sweat from the steamed walls begins to run with frightening rapidity down onto the floor from the places where we are resting our hands against the plaster. And then we hear Mother coming upstairs.

Mother is gentle. She considers innocence to be the supreme virtue. The gaps in the possibility of her successfully raising two sons, without the presence of a father to assert authority and distance, have not yet been made apparent to her. She has a simple vision of reality: everything which is evil she considers to be fiendishly unreal. But she has an overwhelming belief in goodness, as well as a love of it, stronger than her frequent disillusionments; and the strength of that love and belief gives me, while I am still small, a solid basis for character that, despite the ellipses that will come later, nothing will be able to destroy.

She opens the door, expecting to find us bathing, and stands there, looking down at her two sons who are leaning over the back of the tub and dabbling with their washcloths in the dirty water on the floor. We explain that the water sloshed over by chance and that we have gotten most of it up. Then we wait to see what will happen.

Mother has blue eyes and a round face. Sternness is for her a pursing of the lips. And yet we have been warned. The pause comes to an end when I raise my washcloth and wring the dirty water out of it into the tub. She takes the cloth from me and washes it and my brother's in the sink. Then she brings a used towel to dry the floor with and tells us to rinse ourselves with cold water and get out of the tub, quickly, before she loses her temper.

We know that we are saved. But we are to go to the movies in the afternoon and the possibility remains that what we have done will be remembered when the time comes for our departure and we will be kept at home. This would be a tragedy. We go to the movies every Saturday. Besides the Western feature, we see a chapter in a serial, and if you miss a chapter you have no idea what has gone on when you see the next one. We go downstairs quickly, our towels wrapped around us rather than our heavy bathrobes, for it is not really cold, and dress in our bedroom. Then we stand around uncomfortably in odd corners of the living room and dining room, keeping very clean and afraid that anything we do may be used as an excuse to prevent us from being sent off with our fifteen cents each.

And the thing we most long for happens—nothing. Life follows its regular routine. As on every Saturday, we have vegetable soup for lunch. After lunch we are sent out, each with his dime for the movie and his extra nickel for a candy bar.

We return home after having seen only a little bit of the movie a second time, determined not to give displeasure by being late. We eat supper and are sent to bed.

In bed we feel for each other that wonderful friendliness which comes from having been engaged together in a successful adventure. I watch my brother with short smiles. He returns me one. Barricaded by pillows and the covers, we whisper about the movie we have seen. It told, with many scenes of galloping horses, the story of a friend's great sacrifice for his partner. My brother is filled with a longing for adventure. But I am content.

The Full-Length Portrait

☜☜☜ There were nine children in the family who had been raised in the house where we lived. Clark was the oldest of the five brothers and four sisters. Berta came next. Then Tommy, Annie, and Ada. My mother, Louise, was ten years younger than her oldest brother. Her juniors were Herbert, Smith, and the baby of the family, Jasper, born a decade after her.

All of them were handsome and gregarious; all of them married early, and most of them had children by the time I was growing up. The family was large and happy. There was enough money for each to have his own small home and to live his own life. But above everything else, they loved one another and the house they had been brought up in. Mother and Aunt Berta returned there to live, and during those early years all the others visited frequently. On holidays, they came for large dinners, bringing their servants with them and filling the kitchen as full of cooks as the dining room was of guests. All the leaves were put in the enormous table; even so, the meals had to be served in relays. Our cousins overflowed the house, and my brother and I played with them in the yard, initiating them into our secret places, or putting on shows with them on the flat roof of the old chicken house beneath the apple tree. On spring and summer afternoons, bridge parties filled the parlor, library, and living room with women; on autumn and winter weekends, my uncles stopped by on their way to and from hunting trips. In between, plump, laughing, more distant relatives visited for a week at a time, just as they had when my grandparents were alive. Maturity had not separated the brothers and sisters. They were joined by a love closer than that which they found in marriage.

In a sense, their closeness and their gregariousness were a measure of how far they had come from the harsh reality of their parents' and grandparents' world. They believed in the Old Testament morality their mother and father had instilled in them, but their parents' and grandparents' strength had lain in actions, not beliefs. As they grew up, the strictness and bounty of their childhoods reinforced their conventionality; they did not long to conquer new worlds, only to keep the one they knew. I doubt that any one of them ever wanted to be someone other than himself, no matter how different he may have wished his life to be, later on, when money trouble became so great that it separated them from one another for a while. Their lives were as far from the venturous ones of the generations before them as my life was to be from theirs, and although Mother talked more to me about her father and grandfather than she did about my father, I received most of my impressions of them, accurate and inaccurate, from the house itself.

A full-length, life-size portrait of my great-grandfather hung in the entrance hall. It was one of those official paintings that resemble each other more than they resemble the people who sit for them. The man in it wore a sack coat, striped morning trousers, and a watch chain across his chest, and held a tall silk hat in his hand. He wore a stand-up collar of the type common in the seventies but no necktie. The picture was so large that, in addition to the wires suspending its heavy gold frame from the moulding above, two strong metal angles attached to the wall supported it from beneath. Mother called the man in the portrait "Grandpa Smith." He was her mother's father, and when I asked about him she told me this story.

My great-grandfather never wore a necktie, and because the woman he commissioned to do the portrait included a necktie on his likeness he refused to accept it. The artist painted out the necktie, but he remained adamant. She had desecrated his character by portraying him with a piece of ribbon around his neck, he said; she had meddled with the truth, and he was neither going to pay for the picture nor discuss the matter further.

On his way home from this denunciation he stopped at the homeplace. To his daughter he said that the portrait would not look bad in the front hall, and suggested that she go to the studio of the artist who had painted it and offer her a hundred dollars. He was pretty sure, although the original price had been higher, that she could get it for that.

"Your great-grandfather," Mother said, "was a *successful* businessman."

His name was Jasper Newton Smith. He was proud of the Smith, and one of his pastimes was baiting other Smiths who tried to fancy up their surnames with odd spellings or hyphenated additions. He had been born in 1833.

" 'The famous year when the stars fell,' he always called it. But I don't know why," Mother said. "He wasn't educated. He could hardly read and write. He was a self-made man."

He had been born in a rural county in central Georgia, and first came to Atlanta at the end of the Civil War, when the city was a desolation of bricks and ashes. He took one look around him, and, seeing that the only things that had survived the burning of the city were the blackened brick chimneys, he purchased fourteen acres of clayey land for a hundred dollars an acre, in the four-month period between Sherman's departure and the Union occupation, when Confederate currency was almost worthless but still legal tender, and set himself up as a brick manufacturer.

Atlanta became the center of the Reconstruction. Mr. Smith sold millions of bricks. He invested his profits in real estate, and in a few years, without becoming any more educated, he was a rich man.

While he was still at the beginning of this transformation, Mother's father, Thomas Jefferson Donaldson, met him. It was three years after the end of the war. Mr. Smith was thirty-five, and my grandfather was a boy of seventeen. About him, also, Mother told me a story.

For the first two years after the end of the fighting, he worked on his father's farm, which was near Buckhead, on the northern outskirts of Atlanta, and had been in the line of fighting during the Battle of Peachtree Creek. One day when there was money to spare for the first time, he asked his father for enough to buy a suit. His father gave him five dollars, and upon inquiring if that was all he was to get and receiving yes for an answer, my grandfather handed back the five dollars and left home.

For a year he worked as a chain-gang guard nearby in Norcross; then he went to Atlanta and met Mr. Smith. Two years more and he was Superintendent of the Department of Public Works of Fulton County, but his job was not as far removed as it sounds from the one in Norcross. All construction for the county was done by prison labor, and even in my mother's girlhood (and she was the middle one of his children and not to be born for thirty years) he still kept his office at one of the chain-gang camps, rather than at the courthouse, and was less often there than outdoors wherever work was going on.

Mother did not tell me how the two men met, but in those early days the county was an important purchaser of Mr. Smith's bricks. From my grandfather's rapid rise I would even think that he must have been, in some way that was to the older man's advantage, Mr. Smith's protégé. At any rate, the young man and the middle-aged man became friends. Rain made the city, which resembled a Western town, a sea of mud; outdoor work was at times impossible, and on rainy days and at night they played cards at the older man's house. Mr. Smith was married by then, with a family, and when my grandfather first visited their house his future wife, Mr. Smith's older daughter, was three years old. In the evenings, she and her sister sat in their high chairs, listening to the shuffle and tap of cards and watching the games of setback. One night Mr. Smith said, "If you win this evening, I'll give you one of my daughters." My grandfather won. Mr. Smith generously allowed him to choose between Ella, two, and Anna, three. My grandfather selected the latter, and after that, whenever he saw her on her way to school in a gingham dress and with her lunch in a tin box, he would say, "Here comes my little sweetheart." When he was thirty-two and she was eighteen, they were married.

By that time, Mr. Smith was a builder and promoter, a figure in public life; and when, gazing at the portrait in the hall, I asked Mother what he had done, she said impressively:

"He built The House That Jack Built."

This was not the residence in the nursery tale but a business structure in downtown Atlanta. Its celebrity had greatly impressed her in childhood. Mr. Smith was a showman and a pious Baptist as well as a businessman. The House That Jack Built was three stories high and covered all over with marble slabs on which were carved Biblical texts, most of them pointing out the importance of economy.

Mr. Smith's eccentricity had made him a public character by the time Mother was growing up. He sat a good part of each day downtown in the lobby of the Kimball House Hotel, giving his opinions on public figures and controversies, and in time he erected a second building, which became even more famous than The House That Jack Built. The Bachelors' Domain was a residence for men. Each apartment was named after a state of the Union and decorated with the coat of arms and scenes from the history of the state, and it was a rule of the house that no woman could ever be a guest within its doors. However, after his two daughters and his son were married, Mr. Smith sold his home, cavalierly turned the Bachelors' Domain into a regular hotel, and moved into it with his wife.

When he was seventy-three—twelve years before his death, which occurred two years before I was born—he erected another notable structure, a private mausoleum for himself in Oakland Cemetery, on the roof of which, supplementing the full-length portrait in our front hall, was a life-size (and tieless) granite statue of himself seated in a chair. Most of our relatives were buried in another cemetery, and I never visited this one when I was a child. But one Sunday afternoon as Mother, my brother, and I were riding out Fair Street on our way to the Grant Park Zoo with Aunt Ada and her husband, Uncle Felix, the stone figure was pointed out to me, clearly visible against the sky, above the high cemetery wall.

My great-grandfather and my grandfather remained friends throughout their lives, and my grandfather followed Mr. Smith's example in investing most of his money in real estate. Nevertheless, my grandfather's character, in the middle years of his life, was developed largely in opposition to his father-in-law's. Mr. Smith was ostentatious and unashamed of the power of his money. He made presents of silver dollars to his grand-children and gained their affection, but his son-in-law said of him that he cared more for a dollar than for any child who ever lived. My grandfather himself was outwardly matter-of-fact and proper. Everything Mother ever told me about her father pictured him as a man who liked to live as privately as possible. The idea of sitting the afternoon in the lobby of the Kimball House never attracted him—not after sixteen home-less, unmarried years. As far back as she could remember, the table in the dining room saw him in his armchair for all three daily meals—the midday dinner, for which he came home, as well as breakfast and supper. In the evenings, before he ate, he had his toddy, made of sugar and water and North Georgia corn whiskey, in his own parlor; and after supper he played cards, Mr. Smith coming to visit him now. The idea of con-troversy so far from delighted him (as it did his father-in-law) that when a politician, one day on the county courthouse steps, accused him of feeding his family with produce of the county prison farm, he resigned that same afternoon from the job he had held for forty-three years, and withdrew en-tirely into private life.

As much as Mother told me about these two men, the main point did not get through to me: that between them they were almost entirely responsible for the character of the house in which we lived and which I thought of, and continued to think of as long as I lived there, as wholly feminine. Mr. Smith was even responsible for its location, for the ground that the

homeplace stood on was at the edge of the tract he had bought
and used for the manufacture of his bricks; and at the rear
of the side yard, where it dropped off toward the back street,
my brother and I used to play in an open bank of the thick
glutinous clay, as slippery as grease when wet.

Inside the house, the furniture was the type that would have
been chosen by a man determined to put forth the solidity
of his position in the world but not to be as ostentatious as
his father-in-law. The sideboards in the dining room were
presided over by Aunt Berta, and I thought of the sideboards
as hers. But no woman would have bought those heavy pieces
of furniture, with their doored cabinets, their double drawers,
their many-levelled and much carved whatnots, their thickly
bevelled back mirrors. And I learned later, when I asked, that
my grandfather had purchased them out of the bar of the
old Martha Hotel when it was being demolished.

There were two of these sideboards. On one sat the enormous
cut-glass punch bowl and its twelve cut-glass cups, which were
referred to by Mother and my aunt as "Mama's"; but from a
photograph, on Mother's dresser, of my grandmother, taken
toward the end of her life, in which she is wearing an ankle-
length dress of the same gingham she had worn as a girl and
looks almost like a farm wife, I am sure that her husband,
rather than she, bought and treasured them. Much more sug-
gestive of her was the tan-and-white cowhide-seated straight
chair in the kitchen.

The crystal cruet set, the salt and pepper shakers, and sugar
bowl were kept on the other sideboard, the one nearer the

kitchen; and I remember one day finding the sugar bowl half empty and filling it with salt, not out of mischief or to see anyone's discomfort when he used it but because the salt and sugar looked so much alike that I wondered if their difference was not due to the containers they were kept in, and if the salt would not taste like sugar if it were placed in the same bowl and kept there.

In the same way that I was not sure about the difference between the salt and sugar, I was not always sure of the difference between my great-grandfather and my grandfather. Probably from my having heard Mother call the man in the full-length portrait "Grandpa," the two became confused in my mind. Probably, also, this confusion came from the fact that not a single personal relic of my grandfather remained in the house. Possessions of his must have survived his death, six months after I was born, but by the time Mother had returned with my brother and me to live in three of the downstairs rooms, nothing in the house—with the exception of a small oval-framed photograph on the living-room wall—brought my grandfather to mind. None of the personal possessions that Mother and Aunt Berta pictured when they spoke of their father were there for me to see. Mention was made of his roll-top desk, but neither the desk nor his whiskey decanter, neither his pipe nor his tobacco canister remained; and although the chair at the head of the dining-room table was referred to as "Papa's," it differed from the others only by having arms, and my fatherless imagination put no figure there.

Two things finally made real to me these two men and

their relationship to the house in which I had been brought up. In the case of my great-grandfather, it was when I took a volume of the *History of Georgia* out of the glass-doored bookcase in the library one day and read an excerpt from the introduction to a life of him that he had commissioned before he died.

> Jasper Newton Smith is the most unique being in Georgia. So absolutely self-made is he that everything he has said or done leaves the impress of Jasper Newton Smith only. When Nature molded him she broke the die. He has never imitated anybody in anything. Consenting to be himself from boyhood, he has never changed his mind. He is strictly an original and will pass into history as one of the few "originals" who ever lived.

However unpleasant or funny a man with such an opinion of himself—and this was surely Mr. Smith's opinion, if not his words—might have been, it was illuminating to know that such an attitude had been part and parcel of his making the world go round with himself on top, and of his leaving an estate of half a million dollars when he died.

In the case of my grandfather, it was a discovery I made at the time the homeplace was being torn down.

Up until then, Mother had succeeded in conveying only two things to me about this man who built roads for the county and who loved his home—that he was strict and that he was kind. She herself, to the best of her ability, was also; and so these two facts did not do much to make him real. Nor did the illustrations in which she embodied them help much. When she asked to have a new dress and he refused her request, or when, after finishing Miss Hanna's School for Girls, she wanted to take a business course and he refused his permission, there was no pleading or appeals; his word was final. Well, except for the pleading, that was true about her, too. And even though I had heard Uncle Smith say that my grandfather once gave him such a whipping with a board from the crate in which one of Aunt Berta's wedding presents arrived that he could never see a wedding present without thinking of a beating—well, both Mother and Aunt Berta gave whippings, too. Nevertheless, I knew that by those two words "strict" and "kind," and the tone in which she said them, she meant to convey something formidable and masculine, something that I did not know and could not even imagine.

My discovery was in a transparent safe in the attic. The frame of the safe was iron, the six walls of thick plate glass. It was in a far corner; probably no one had thought of it since it had been put there; and in it I found a lined pencil tablet containing the draft of a letter by my grandfather.

Atlanta, Georgia
July 1, '89

To the Honorable Board of Commissioners of Roads and Revenues of Fulton County:

This morning between day light and sun up I received a telephone message from the South Atlantic Camp stating that the prisoners at the Camp (67 in number) had refused to go to their work and would not leave the prison building. I went immediately to the camp and found them in a state of mutiny, utterly refusing to obey any order or listen to any reasoning.

I went into the building and asked what was the matter. Some of them wanted concessions of one kind and some of another, and most of them of a reasonable nature. The majority had refused to eat their breakfast and had thrown it all over the building, stating that they would not eat fat meat and corn bread and syrup for breakfast. Some of them wanted me to discharge some of the guards, saying that they had a new boss and wanted new guards. Some of them wanted to receive company on Sundays, and some of them wanted to be carried to another camp, while others said that they did not think they had been treated right for the last few months.

There were about fifteen or so that took a leading part in this affair and had armed themselves with pieces of their bunks, sides and legs of the stove, and bottles filled with syrup. They had formed themselves in a line across the aisle of the building in front of the door and told the others that they would kill the first prisoner that tried to go to work. Some of the men had started to go and they had knocked one of them down and said that they would kill any other prisoner that started or any boss or guard that undertook to come into the building.

I could not reason with them to any effect. They utterly refused to listen to anything in the shape of reasoning or orders. So, when I had exhausted all motions, I took a pair of handcuffs and went to the ringleader and told him to put up his hands and he refused, but I succeeded in getting them on him after he had made considerable resistance, and found him armed with an open knife and long strips of timber which he had torn from a bunk. I took him outside the building into the stockade and hit him fifteen lashes with a strap made for that purpose, at the end of which he said that he would go to his work and would not make any more trouble while he stayed in the camp.

I then proceeded to take out twelve more of the ring-leaders and hit them from eight to fifteen lashes, stopping when they agreed to go to work and make no more trouble. . . .

This letter made the man Mother had spoken of—a man who was strict and kind to his children, and yet who, by the very force of his presence, could confuse an armed and rebellious convict and disarm him—as real to me as the upholstered marquetry chairs and settees, the mahogany and oak pedestals in the library and parlor, the sideboards in the dining room, and the beds in the bedrooms. The world that lay behind the house, from which it was a refuge and to which it was an ornament, became visible; and the house itself, as well as the childhoods and early lives of my uncles and aunts, appeared for the first time in relation to the events of political and financial struggle, lasting from the end of the Civil War through the beginning of the century, which I had read of at school. But by that time, the house had ceased to exist, and all through the years when I lived there, the turn-of-the-century world that it was a part of was no more alive to me than the official oil-and-canvas figure of my great-grandfather in the full-length portrait, or the photograph of my grandfather in the small oval frame on the living-room wall.

The Ring:
A Link in a Chain

⊂⊇⊂⊇⊂⊇ The boy who lived next door in the brick house on the other side from the McCrareys was named Wade. He had a printing set which consisted of a metal box containing a set of rubber letters and a grooved wooden block for setting the letters in. In the top of the box there was a pad for inking the letters. The wooden block was not large and only six lines of type could be set at a time, but this was sufficient for the business that Wade and I were planning. At the five-and-ten-cents store, we bought a pack of plain white cards the size of calling cards. Then we went about the neighborhood, taking orders for names to be printed on them, business or personal.

The sample we prepared was neat. We were earnest in our effort to obtain orders, marching together from the Gulf filling station to the Wise Dry Cleaning Shop, from the Colonial Florist to King's Hardware Store. Our prices were modest, only twice what the plain cards had cost, and as it was a friendly neighborhood, we received several orders. We returned to Wade's house and set to work. It was Wade's printing set and he had advanced the money for the cards. I did the printing. When I made a mistake, Wade became nervous and wanted to take over. But as soon as the next card was printed his anxiety was gone. When the work was finished, he and I looked at it proudly and set out to deliver the orders.

We had lived next door to each other as long as we could remember, and our families were acquainted in the way families are who have nearness in common and little else. At the time the newer of the two houses had been built, both families had been well off. But in our lifetime, Wade's family had become wealthier and mine had not. The difference was apparent in the states of the two properties. Wade's front lawn was kept green and trim by a chauffeur-yardman. Ours was an uneven and dusty expanse in which dandelions outnumbered the tufts of grass. Even where there was grass, it was a different color from that in Wade's yard. The verdure tended by the yardman was bright green, while the other was dull and dark, the color of the weathered house behind it.

The presents Wade received on his birthdays were a cross-section of the new games and toys that were in the stores. There were so many in the sewing room upstairs where they were stored, and on the sleeping porch where we played when we were in his house, that no toy could hold attention for long. The accurately detailed fire engine would be abandoned in the middle of a trip for the cork-shooting popgun. The gun and its gallery of tropical birds, with long tails which popped over backwards when their heads were hit, so that the bright colors of their fronts disappeared into the pale wood of their backs, would be abandoned in the middle of someone's turn for the erector set. And the erector set would be abandoned for the tinker toys.

I was given presents on my birthdays, but they were different. The one I valued most was a gold signet ring that had been my mother's when she was a girl. The ring was an adult's possession, not a child's. It was made of eighteen carat gold and was a present to be kept always, not played with for a season and then thrown away. It was large for my ring finger; I wore it on the index finger of my right hand. Even there it was loose enough to turn easily and it could be slipped off without effort. Mother was afraid that I might lose it. But I was too proud of the ring to let it slip off unawares.

I wore the ring when we went to deliver the cards. Ink had dirtied it, along with everything else, while we were printing. I had taken it off and cleaned it with my handkerchief when I washed my hands and had put it back on. The blue stains on my fingers remained, only a little lighter than they had been before they were washed. But the ring was spotless. The cards also, except for one or two there were fingerprints on, were unsoiled. Wade wrapped them in folded pieces of fancy paper that he found in the trash basket in his mother's bedroom. Then we left the sleeping porch and its toys and proceeded down the stairs, out of the house, and along the walk that divided the perfectly kept lawn.

The total profit, which Wade carried when we had collected for our orders and started back home, was sixty cents. As we neared his house, he became thoughtful. There was nothing in the entire printing process that he could not have done by himself if he had wanted to. And all the investment had been his. At the front steps, he said that he had to go upstairs. I suggested that we should divide the money first. The money was not to be divided, Wade replied. The printing set and the ink and the cards had been his. And so was the profit.

He went inside. I faced toward home, and by the time I had gone through the hedge that separated the two front driveways my eyes were filled with tears. The thirty cents that I had been planning to spend did not exist. But it was not the loss of the money, it was the total surprise with which the loss had come that made the lump rise in my throat, tighten the muscles of my face, and come out in tears. I had not imagined the thoughts that were in Wade's mind as we were returning home. His betrayal was as unexpected as a slap in the face.

Mother discovered my tears and I told her what had happened. She telephoned next door. But when Wade's mother learned what had happened she sided with her son. She was glad, she said, for me to come over and play with Wade, but she did not see that this entitled me to half the profits from what Wade did. That was not the way matters were arranged in life. And that was not the way they should be arranged with children, either.

Mother told me to forget what Wade had done; she would give me some money, a dime, and she sent me out into the back yard to play. There, sitting in the shade of an oak tree between the house and the woodpile, I amused myself by pushing a stick through the dust and pretending that it was a train going from city to city. Mother looked out once or twice to make sure I was there. Then she had other things to do. Late in the afternoon, tired of playing, I walked back toward the barn.

During my play I had forgotten what had happened. Pretence had completely absorbed me. But my mind came back to it as I walked. The unacceptable thing was that Wade cared more for the money than for me. Neither my mother, nor Wade's, seemed to understand that. I did not wholly understand it myself. Wade had been happy while we were doing the work and going to deliver the cards. So had I. And then suddenly I had been turned away as though I were an intruder who was trying to take something that was not my own.

I could not accept it. I would never have acted toward Wade in the same manner, and my mind came up against a blank wall when it tried to grasp that this was the way people acted toward one another. Adults condemned when anyone fought or stole, and comforted the victim. This was worse and I could not believe that they understood how I had been hurt or they would not treat the event so lightly. Their misunderstanding doubled my pain, and I longed to be able to do something to make others understand and to relieve my isolation.

At the back of the yard, near a small cottonwood tree, a board was missing in the fence. Through the opening, you could see and talk to a person in the next yard. When I reached the open space, Wade was on the other side, bouncing a volley ball against the brick wall of the garage at the back of his family's house. He bounced it for a while, pretending not to know that I was watching him. Then he turned to the opening and challenged:

"You can't come into my yard, but I can go into yours if I want to."

When this received no reply, he added:

"Only children who have no family pride print cards for money."

"Then how come you did it?"

"It was your idea."

"Then the money's half mine."

Wade bounced the ball, his fat body shaking each time his arm struck downward. Then he said:

"I can't go into your yard, either, but if you'll walk to the corner with me I'll buy us an ice cream cone. You won't tell if I cut across your yard, will you?"

"Come ahead."

Wade stepped through the open space where the board was missing. He smelled of soiled underwear: to me the odor summed up all that I refused to accept. I clenched my fist and struck. Wade struck back. Standing at the side of the opening, we battled. At the first blow that hit Wade's face, tears began to flow from his eyes. He rushed forward, clawing and pushing. One of his hands grabbed the hand I wore my ring on. I pulled off the ring and threw it on the ground.

"Look what you've done," I cried.

We stood facing one another.

"You pulled my mother's ring off my finger."

"I didn't."

"You did."

"I didn't mean to."

"You did."

People arrived from the houses. Wade was taken home. I kneeled to the ground and began to look for the ring. I had not yet recovered it when my brother was sent from the house to tell me that I must come indoors to supper.

Vegetables and sometimes flowers had been planted at the back of the lot. Weeds and vines grew there, and the soil was uneven. In the after-supper twilight, on my hands and knees, I searched in the weeds in front of the fence where the board was missing. The ring might have rolled or I might have thrown it harder than I realized. But I found only thorns, stones, soil. With rising fear, I went back to the bare center of earth in hope that the ring would be in the very spot where I had looked so many times, and that at last I would see it. When I did not, I began to turn over loose clods and to dig in the ground. People had been indignant against what they thought Wade had done, but that was faint comfort in the fading light. Once it was night, what was lost might never be found; the search I had begun might never end.

And suddenly I could no longer see. The space about me near the ground had become darker than the sky. The twilight was seeping out of the black weed stalks and gray soil, blinding the air to a man's height above the earth where the ring was lost; and high above, the same color as the still bright sky, the first star had come out.

The Blond Bed

⇇⇇⇇On spring afternoons, when I was eight or nine and my cousin Carl was seventeen or eighteen, he used, after having spent the morning dressed in gym shorts, practicing javelin throwing in the side lot, to lie in the swing on the front porch and study. He was freshly bathed, wearing clean cotton-khaki trousers and an open shirt. His knees were propped up and a bare stretch of hairy leg showed between his white socks and the tan cuffs of his trousers. While he was lying there, I took great pleasure in sneaking up and grabbing his pencil, or giving the swing a push, or jerking one of the hairs out of his leg. Naturally, when I did this he grabbed at me, and the fear of being caught by him filled me with joy. As fast as I could, I rushed to the front steps and down into the yard. Then, if I was not chased, I waited awhile and, stooping down so that I could not be seen from the swing, stole around to the steps that were on the side of the house, at the far end of the porch, and watched him from there.

Sometimes when I bothered him, instead of reaching out and trying to catch me, my cousin would jump up from the swing and chase me a few steps, and sometimes he would shout for me to go away and leave him alone. But if he was in a good mood, he would lie with his algebra or trigonometry book held in one hand against his knees, his other hand resting inert across his stomach or along the wooden edge of the swing, and pretend to be lost in concentration on the page he was studying. I realized, then, that his strategy was to feign unawareness in order to catch me. Cautiously, at a safe distance, still breathing heavily from my exhaustion and inhaling the odor of the pear tree in bloom in the side yard, or the bed of jonquils and narcissus that grew near the side steps, I would wait at the far end of the porch until I saw some convincing sign of unawareness on his part. Then I would creep forward again.

I knew what would happen if he caught me. He would hold me with my arm twisted behind my back until I promised to go away and leave him alone. He never hurt me, not even when he was angry. His anger took the form of curtly warning me that he was not in the mood for playing and that I was to cut it out. This was defeat to me, for it meant that the game was over, and after it was over there was no relationship between us.

A black leather couch, tufted into diamond shapes by deep-set black buttons, stood in the living room. It had neither arms nor back, and it curved up at one end. One day, when my cousin was lying on it, reading the newspaper, I tried a new amusement. It was unusual for him to be in that part of the house. Perhaps he was there to escape a house cleaning or a party. He was lying as he did on the swing, but with his legs stretched out, and he held the open newspaper in both hands in front of his face. Creeping up to the foot of the couch, I threw myself full length on him and began to flick the back of the newspaper. I thumped it gently at first, then harder, testing how far I could go before he protested. In between thumps, I waited. He let the thumps go on longer than I would have expected. Then, suddenly, I won. He threw the newspaper aside, grabbed me, and tickled me in my ribs until I was screaming and weeping with laughter.

These were isolated incidents. We had little to do with each other. Yet I was not conscious of missing the friendship of my cousin. My interest must have gone underground and come out in the form of an attachment to the furniture in his bedroom. For years later, the bed began to appear in my dreams.

And it was different from any other bed I had ever seen. All the other beds in the homeplace were heavy carved oak or mahogany, with high solid foots and heads, stained dark brown or red. This one bed was blond. Its foot and head were screens of delicate open work, resembling spools of bamboo. The poles of the screen were of various lengths, like organ pipes, ending in horizontal ledges at different levels. The design was probably oriental, but in childhood the word "oriental" suggested black and brightly colored lacquer designs to me, and nothing could have been plainer than these simply carved rods and their corn husk color. A various-levelled dressing table, with a cabinet set high up on one side, above a low shelf, and a chest of drawers of the same blond wood, were also in the room.

Occasionally when I knew that my cousin was out of the

house, I would slip upstairs to his room at the front end of the long hall and prowl around. I was like an animal on the scent. I did not know what I was looking for. I would sniff the bed covers and lift the discarded clothes I found thrown across a chair, or I would open the cabinet at the top of the dressing table and look at the cuff-links, the razor and shaving brush and styptic stick stored there. I walked through the room very quietly, observing as I almost never observed at that time, consciously taking in details as though I were a traveler memorizing the ruins of some lost civilization I had discovered and would have to carry back in my mind to the inhabited world. When I heard someone coming, I slipped out, charged with more energy than I had had before I entered, satisfied, somehow, by the intake of excitement rather than by the release of it. But my cousin and I never became friends. I did not learn any ordinary everyday thing from him. And even so simple an action as tying my shoe I did backward, in the reverse of the procedure a boy learns from watching a man, for I learned from seeing Mother tie my shoe when it was on my foot and she was facing me.

A Coin

with a Hole in It

⊂⊃⊂⊃⊂⊃Early each summer, Mother and Aunt Berta (as their father had before them) took advantage of low prices and ordered a railway carload of coal, which was stored in the "coal house"—a big enclosed space under the servants' room, behind the kitchen. You entered the coal house from the back yard— and the coal filled it almost to the door. But on the right, where the axe leaned against the wall, enough room remained for kindling to be stacked. Aunt Berta did not always find it easy to persuade my cousin to cut kindling when she wanted it, and so she and Mother decided to fill this space with as much wood as possible during the summer, and to keep it in reserve for the periods when the old Negro who cut kindling for us did not show up. There was no question of buying wood, for we had a large woodpile, only of finding someone to cut it.

One afternoon a stranger, dressed in clean faded dungarees and a brown plaid work shirt, stopped at the house and asked for work. He was lean. His age was about that of my youngest uncle. And Mother and Aunt Berta decided that he looked less like a tramp than like a country boy. His mouth was sharply drawn, the whites of his eyes were clear, and he had long, sunburned muscles, none of which went with a shiftless or drinking character. Besides, their brother, Smith, who had had a quarrel with his wife and had spent the night at the house, was still there, so they were not afraid. They told the stranger that there was no real work to be done but that if he would go to the woodpile in the back yard and cut some kindling they would give him something to eat.

The woodpile was a stack of blackened lumber, half covered by weeds. It had accumulated from the collapse of a number of buildings. First the doghouse and the fence around the dog yard had been pulled down. Then the chicken house. Finally, part of the barn. None of these had been demolished deliberately; they had simply sagged toward the earth until my brother and I, or our cousins, knocked them over in play, and the loose boards had been cleaned up and moved to this spot, which was away from the corrugated-tin garage and yet near enough to the house to be handy for firewood.

Aunt Berta took the coal-house key from the nail in the kitchen where it hung, attached by a string to a long narrow piece of wood, and went out with it to the back yard, where the young man was waiting. She unfastened the padlock on the door of the coal house, opened the heavy wooden door, and pointed out the axe. The young man said "Yes, ma'am" to each of her statements and smiled a smile that showed his teeth, very pale and even. Then he went to the woodpile and began to split beams, raising the axe all the way over his head and twisting his body in an arc at each swing.

I was sitting at the top of the back steps, watching him, when Uncle Smith came out of the house. He was not yet thirty, but his waist was already going to fat. Frowning at the sudden light, he stopped beside me and said, "Well, you look pretty damned busy."

I did not reply and he asked, "What do you think you're doing?"

I said that I was doing nothing.

"Nothing just about to hell covers it."

Again I did not say anything. The only sound was that of the axe against wood.

"How old are you?"

I told him.

"When I was your age," he said, "I could cut all the wood needed here, and my daddy saw that I damned well did it."

With a loud "huh," he went on down the steps and across the yard to the garage, where he had left his automobile the night before. I went indoors until I saw his car turn from the driveway into the street. Then I came out again by the front door and went around to the back yard.

It was a warm day. The sun was solid and bright, casting shadows beneath the oak trees, and in the open lighting up the green weeds that grew beyond the woodpile. When I came around the corner of the house, I saw that the man had stopped to wipe the perspiration from his forehead with the sleeve of his shirt. He saw me, smiled, and asked where he could get a drink of water.

I showed him an outdoor faucet at the side of the back steps. As he crossed to it, he asked me if the person who had left was my father. I told him that he was my uncle—my father did not live with us and I did not know where he was.

While the man was drinking, leaning over, and letting the water run into his mouth, Mother called me into the kitchen and Lily Mae gave me a plate of food for him. He took it and sat down on the ground, in the shade of the largest oak tree, with his back against the tree trunk, and I wandered away and pretended to be interested in the yard.

Halfway between the blackened beams of the woodpile and the sandy track that automobile tires and water from the broken rain pipe at the corner of the house had made diagonally across the yard, there were two round flower beds filled with marigolds, California poppies, and larkspur.

The man, pointing to them as he ate, asked, "Who made those?"

I told him that I had made one and my brother the other.

"I bet I can tell you how you did it." He took another bite of corn bread, then continued, "First, you laid an automobile tire down flat on the ground. Next, you dug up the dirt inside it, and then dug up some more dirt somewhere else and filled the tire with it. Then you took the tire away and put that circle of stones where it was."

He described the process exactly as though he had been there watching when I had made the flower bed, or as though he had been listening when Aunt Winnie had told me how to make it. My surprise was obvious, and he smiled.

"My mother used to make them the same way," he said. "We lived in the country, in a place very different from here. There weren't any trees or any grass, just dust everywhere. But my mother kept one flower bed like those on each side of the house. And she drew up a bucketful of water for them each evening, no matter how much my old man objected to her using the water."

That had been a long time ago, he said. I did not know how long a long time meant to him, but in the silence that followed, as he took another mouthful of meat and corn bread, I imagined the time stretching around him as bare and dusty as the ground he had described. Then he smiled again and asked me if I had ever seen the ocean.

I told him that we had been to the seashore in Florida when I was small and we lived with my father but that I did not remember it; and since we had returned to Atlanta I had never been farther away than to visit my father's sister, who lived in the country, in the opposite direction from the ocean.

"I think you'd like the ocean," he told me. "You ought to go and see it sometime. It's bigger than you can imagine. I've shipped all the way to China, and you don't see anything but water, all the way to the horizon all around you, for three weeks at a time. You'd like Japan and China, too. Osaka and Shanghai and Ningpo."

I had never heard these last names, or even any like them. I stood grinning at the stranger. Then he made a funny little yapping noise, like a Pekinese, and said, "That's 'I'll never forget you' in Japanese."

As I listened, I felt as I did when the rain or the night changed the familiar landscape of the back yard into a place as different from its usual self as a foreign city would be—an alien feeling that seemed in some odd way to connect me to the stranger. Since he had left his ship in San Francisco, he said, he had come back across the southern end of the country, hitchhiking or riding freight all the way. The names of the places he mentioned were almost as unfamiliar to me as the place names of the Orient. In Texarkana he had stopped to see his family, but when he reached the farm where he had lived no one was there. The doors and windows were all open. There was not a stick of furniture in the small house. And of the flower beds on either side of the yard there remained only the bare circles of stone.

After a pause, he smiled again and added, "I'm going to the East Coast now and take a ship and see what the Atlantic looks like."

He gave me the plate and I took it inside. When I came out again, he was working once more, cutting up an old cedar fence post that was yellow toward the outside and red in the center and that filled the air with a strong fragrance. He called to me:

"Come and watch me and I'll show you how to split kindling."

The post had already been cut into lengths and he was chopping up the short, thick pieces. He did it carefully, and I stood just outside the range of the swinging axe and watched the wood somersault up into the air and straight back to earth as, with single blows, he split the lengths into halves, the halves into quarters, the quarters into eighths.

When he was finished, the two of us stacked the kindling into a neat pile in the corner of the coal house, near the door; then I went inside and told my mother that the man was ready to go. We came out onto the back porch and found him at the faucet, washing his face and hands. Mother had prepared a sack of sandwiches for him to take with him, like the sacks she prepared for my brother and me when we went to school. Aunt Berta, who went out to the coal house and locked the door, was pleased with the amount of work he had done and told me to come inside with her. She hung the key to the coal house on its nail and handed me a quarter to give him.

I hurried out to the back porch again, but he was no longer at the water faucet, and when I had gone down the steps to the ground, I could not find him anywhere in the yard. I ran across the sandy automobile tracks and up the unpaved driveway, anxious and bewildered. Then I saw him, framed in the posts of the gate that separated the front from the back yard, walking slowly, ready to turn from the driveway onto the sidewalk.

In his hand he carried his tan sweater, as he had when he arrived at the house; and when I called to him and he turned and looked at me, I saw that his brown hair, wet from his wash, lay unnaturally dark and formal along his forehead. I gave him the quarter. He thanked me. For a moment we stood smiling at each other. Then he drew his hand from his pocket and held it out to me. In the palm there was a round, copper-colored coin with a square hole in it. He asked if I knew what it was. I shook my head.

"It's a cash," he said. "A Chinese coin. I brought it back with me, and I'd like to give it to you to remember me by. It isn't worth anything here, but whenever you look at it you'll think of me."

A straw sewing basket, on which a design was stitched in red and blue wool, sat on Mother's dresser in the back bedroom. At the top, to lift the lid by, the threads held a coin like the one the stranger had given me; and when I showed the cash to my brother and told him what it was, he did not believe that the man had brought it back from a foreign country. It was probably an ornament off a sewing basket like Mother's, he said, and even if I got to China it would be of no value.

But for once I did not believe him. When I looked at the copper-colored coin, I thought of the vagrant's brown plaid shirt; of how, on the inside, where the sleeve was rolled up, I had seen the plaid pattern repeated in a lighter tan the same shade as his face, as though the sun at the same time that it had faded his shirt had darkened his skin until the two met. The color joined with the brown fading snapshots of my father in our family photograph album, snapshots of places as flat and strange as the foreign names the stranger had used—stretches of sand at Daytona Beach, or level fields in pine woods cleared for growing pineapples. Between the shirt and the photographs there was the copper-colored coin in my hand. And somehow, out of the combination of all three, emerged the exact shade of my own longing and belief.

The Bath Tub—II

It is summer, warm weather; the blinds of the bathroom window are folded back into the casements, the window is open; but it is still necessary to heat water downstairs on the kitchen stove and to carry it upstairs to the bathroom if my brother and I are to be clean after we bathe, and we are once again in the tub together. I am sitting in the back, as before, and my brother is in front of me, but he is acting exactly as though he is bathing alone. There are no games, no conversation. And when I want the soap, which is in the rack hung over the porcelain rim of the tub in front of him, he will neither hand it to me nor allow me to reach over him and take it. He has asked to be allowed to bathe alone; Mother has refused his request; and he has decided to assert his will by pretending that I am not there. But I will not let him. I do not see why I should sit at the back of the tub, unable to wash, and wait until he has finished bathing, especially as when he wants to rinse himself he runs cold water into the tub, considerably increasing the rapidity with which the water we are sitting in is losing its heat. I persist in trying to reach over the barrier of the arm he has raised to prevent me from taking the soap. His only further defense of his privacy is to hit me.

For quite a while now my presence has been an annoyance to him. In the afternoons after school, where we both go although I am two grades behind him, a group of boys from his class gathers at our house to play ball in the side yard. Because of my age, I am a less good player than the others, and my brother defends himself against the drawback of being associated with me by treating me with open contempt before the others have a chance to. There is no reason for him to put himself out to keep my admiration, which he already has, and there is no end to the admiration he wants to win in the unconquered world he is beginning to live in.

This desire has already caused him to join The Boy Scouts of America and to win merit badge after merit badge. For a while, Mother wanted me to join, too; and he was perfectly willing that I should become a boy scout. It would do me a world of good, there was no doubt of that, in his opinion. But he was uneasy the Friday night that he was first to take me to a meeting. I was pleased to go; but I knew most of the boys who were members, by sight at least; the club house was only a block from the school where I went every day; and it did not seem to me that I was entering a wholly new world where I would be judged for the first time. But it did to my brother, and he felt that the judgment would reflect on him. He made so many objections that evening to the way I was to be dressed, how my hair was to be combed, and how I was in general to be forced *not* to look peculiar (I looked just as I did on any other occasion when I was clean and my hair was wet and flat) that I saw for the first time how worthless I was in his eyes, not for anything I did or for any skill I lacked, but for the very fact of my existence as what I was, his brother two years younger than he, of whom he was contemptuous. The hurt that evening turned back into myself any desire I might have had to become a boy scout (just as those rejections on the ball field curtailed any proficiency I might have developed in pitching, catching, batting) and began a distance between us which was to become even greater than that he hoped for.

But on this day, while we are in the tub together, it is impossible for him to find any justification for the intimacy that is forced on him. His only defense is in pretending to be alone, and when I insist on reaching over him for the soap he strikes me as hard as he can. I strike back. But the match is not at all even. In none of these encounters have I ever won, and it is not long before I am shedding tears and calling for help.

This is a difficult period for Mother; our conduct bewilders her; and when she arrives in the bathroom she does not know what to do. Circumstances are beginning to prove that her devoting her whole life to her children does nothing to fill the gaps in her authority and in our characters. We return sufficient love to her. Perhaps even too much. But this only increases her helplessness. She cannot control us without violence. And in a feminine world violence is always hysterical.

"All right," she says, "this is the last time! I've warned you enough! Finish bathing and dry yourselves and wait for me here!"

After she has gone, my brother's eyes blaze with hatred. His cheek at the corner of his nose lifts in a sneer which says more eloquently than any words how much he loathes me. I am a snivelling little crybaby, and if only I had not been there he would have been happy. Now there is going to be trouble and I am to blame.

I stand with my eyes on the floor, unable to look at the sneer that makes his face hideous. I, too, feel that everything would have been all right if only he had behaved differently, if he at least had been fair enough to let me use the soap even though he would not speak to me; I mutter that it is not my fault, that it is his fault. He does not deign to answer.

Mother returns, in her hand a switch made of a branch she has broken from one of the small peach trees in the yard. My brother is first. Blindly, as though she is achieving some kind of oblivion through her action, she switches his legs below the knees, demanding with each blow that he promise this is the last time this will happen. After his weeping promise, my turn comes. The blows of the switch burn like fire. I weep and promise, too. But my tears are less full than my brother's. I have already felt the depth of my grief.

When Mother sees the raw red welts she has raised in strips on the backs of our calves, she kneels between us and, there in the bathroom, wraps her arms about my brother and me and bursts into tears, as hurt as we are by what she has done. Her heart fills with remorse; she begs us to love one another. And we say that we will. But there is neither remorse nor love in my brother's eyes.

The Long Sunday Ride

⫅⫅⫅Every Sunday morning, Mother went to All Saints'
Episcopal Church and my brother and I to the Sunday school.
On Sunday afternoons, we often took long automobile rides,
ending with supper at the Yellow Jacket Restaurant. Mr. Dickinson, a man Mother had known before her marriage, and who
paid her visits now that she was divorced, carried us in his car.
He and Mother sat on the front seat of the two door sedan, my
brother and I on the back.

One Sunday in early summer, like many others past and to
come, our drive took us out Peachtree Street, past Buckhead on
the Roswell Road, and back by Northside Drive and Hemphill
Avenue to the restaurant, which was near Georgia Tech. This
route encompassed the two extremes you could see in Atlanta,
slums and mansions, suburbs and country, railroad yards and
crepe myrtle lined drives, spread out between the rolling earth
and flat sky. There was nothing unexpected in these sights. They
made us feel comfortable, proprietory. Part of the trip was on

66

a back road where one of my great aunts lived. Mother had told me that this was where she used to ride in a billy goat cart when she was a girl, and now on each drive I said wasn't this where she used to ride in the goat cart and she said yes. Farther along, there was one of the convict camps from which my grandfather used to work prisoners when he was building roads for the county. And a little farther still, the old people's home, always pointed out with a quiet awe.

These small back roads, lined with trees and too unfrequented to have been widened and repaved, were rollback constructions of black tar that had been built by my grandfather in the first years of the century. The number of leaves that passed the windows of the automobile on these back ways was endless, dizzying in the steadiness with which they continued, and the roads went up and down so rhythmically that I sometimes had a sensation of still moving even after the car had stopped. A foretaste of this sensation would make me feel trapped and restless while the car was moving, and when I felt this way, unless something happened to draw me out of myself, I longed for the ride to be over.

On the road near my great aunt's house this Sunday, we ran over a snake. We did not see it until it was almost under the automobile and we thought that the wheels went over it, but we did not stop to get out and make sure.

I wanted to go back and see if we had killed the snake. I was not anxious for it to be either alive or dead. My feeling about snakes was ambivalent. I was frightened of them and curious about them. But as I looked out of the back window, we turned

from the small road to a larger one and were on our way across
Nancy Creek to Sardis Cemetery. Mother said that even if the
snake had been run over it would live until sundown. This increased my interest. Then Mr. Dickinson said that we would
stop and see the snake on our way back. The ride suddenly had
a point, and when we drew up at the side of the cemetery, the
day had gained an interest it had not possessed before.

It was a windy day, the kind on which the sun is bright and
each object clearly detailed, but the air is cool. The old, crooked
headstones and low cement walls stood out sharply in the sunshine. Between the graves, the tall grass was bending and swaying in the wind. No wall protected the cemetery from the road.
You simply parked at the side of the pavement and walked up
the bank. And the space between the plots was not well kept,
but was like some back yard crossed by paths full of weeds and
the discarded frames of wreathes and flower containers, purple
maypops blooming among them.

First, Mother walked around the Donaldson Brothers &
1898 vault, where her mother and father and some of her uncles
were buried. Then, when she had pulled out a few weeds that
were growing through the cracks in the cement walk around the
stone building, we left and drove farther from town, toward the
Chattahoochee River. The road we took crossed the river on
an old steel girder bridge, painted silver and floored with loose
boards that rumbled as we crossed them, making such a noise
that it sounded as though the whole structure were going to fall
into the muddy water. The river was our destination. We parked
beside some boarded-up cabins, across the road from an inn.

My brother and I got out and walked a little. Then we started back.

My thoughts were on the snake. Promises of any kind meant a great deal to me. In the midst of everyday commonplaces, possibility was the one exciting thing, the one thing that extended the limitations of the familiar, and my interest attached itself enthusiastically to anything that was to be in the future. But I did not like to force the events that were to happen. Particularly, I did not like to ask for what I had been promised.

We started back by Northside Drive. In a part of the country where all the roads twist and turn like the path of a moving snake, Northside Drive is straight. It is paved with white cement. From the top of one long hill, you can see its bright ribbon going far down the hill and far up the next hill, and over it out of sight. Perhaps it was because we never started on this road and only took it on the return trip, when I was tired of riding, but the sight of it always intensified the trapped feeling I had, in the automobile, of being carried along against my will.

I looked forward to the moment when we would turn off Northside Drive and make our way back to the twisting side road we had started on. At each cross road, I thought: This will be where we turn. And when we did not, I thought: It will be the next road. I was reluctant to mention the promise. It was so consistently in my thoughts that I did not think it possible that anyone else had forgotten it. And when, at last, I did mention it, it was too late.

"Oh, it's past now," Mr. Dickinson said. "And it's time to eat. Aren't you hungry?"

"I want to see if the snake is dead."

"You don't care about snakes," my brother said. "You're afraid of them."

"All three of us want to eat," Mother said. "You're the only one who wants to see the snake. You don't want three people to do something they don't want to do, just to please one person, do you?"

I did not answer.

"Do you?"

"No."

I tried not to look at my mother and not to look out of the window or into the interior of the automobile either. I did not want to give in to her, and I did not want her to give in to me. I wanted us to want the same thing. I would have liked to have seen the snake, and I would have liked to have ceased wanting to see the snake. But I was no more able to fulfill the one desire than the other. I wished that as soon as we had left the river I had mentioned returning the way we had come. But it had not occurred to me then that my desire was different from that of the others. And, even if it had, I would not have wanted to separate myself from them further by reminding them of what I wanted. It embarrassed me to think that all the while no one else had wanted what I wanted and that I had not known it. I hated being separated. Yet how could I have known that what I wanted would separate me? And how could I, at someone else's word, now want something else?

"If you sulk," Mr. Dickinson said, "you won't have any appetite for supper."

"I'm not sulking."

"Good. Then I bet we'll have to order you a double-decker, toasted ham and cheese sandwich, won't we?"

"No."

"Oh, I bet we will."

"You'll change your mind when we get to the restaurant," Mother said.

"And I bet we'll have to order you an ice cream sundae for dessert, too," Mr. Dickinson coaxed.

We were coming into the city. Blocks of houses passed, as depressing as the pavement of the street they lined, and vacant lots of weeds and signboards, all of which had the frustrated air of man's most self-wounding destructions. I could not answer. It seemed unfair to me that they were changing the subject and trying to make it a matter of eating and of selfishness on my part. At North Avenue, as we turned and drove past the trees and lawns and red brick buildings of the Georgia Tech campus, and past the shabby frame houses facing it, my misery became so great that I wanted to have neither sight, nor hearing, nor any other sensation.

"I can already smell the melting butter, can't you?" Mr. Dickinson asked.

Mother said:

"Don't tease him."

We had parked on Spring Street, around the corner from the restaurant. I pushed myself as far as possible into the corner of the seat and closed my eyes. I knew what was coming and I wished that it would not happen. But I did not know how to

avoid it. I did not want to stay in the car and be coaxed to go
any more than I wanted to go into the restaurant with them.
I wanted to be somewhere else, by myself, in a different situation. And if pure force of will could have made me, I would
have vanished. Nevertheless, it did not occur to me to get out
of the car and flee. Outside myself, I did not know where to go.
There was nothing I could do but withdraw into myself as far
as I could.

The others had descended from the automobile and were
holding the door open.

"We're going in to eat now. Come on."

"I'm not hungry."

"Come and sit with us, anyway."

"No."

"All right. If you don't want to, we won't make you."

They stood at the side of the automobile a moment longer,
hoping that the idea of being left alone would make me follow
them. Then their footsteps died away.

I opened my eyes. There was a great relief in being alone. And
with the relief came a shame at having acted as I had acted. I
wished that I had not felt as I had felt, and that I had gone
into the brightly lighted restaurant with them and was eating
at one of the shining, white-topped tables. There was nothing
that I liked more than the Yellow Jacket's ham and cheese sandwiches on white bread, toasted in some way that it never was
toasted at home, with a smoothly glazed golden crust outside,
and a wonderful caramel smell of burnt butter. But it had not
been possible for me to think of this until I was by myself.

I looked at the empty interior of the automobile, at the tree-shaded sidewalk that ran between the side of the automobile and the unlighted windows of a store in the same building as the restaurant, and at the thick green leaves of the oaks and elms swaying gently in the evening breeze. It was so quiet that I could hear the clicking on and off of the traffic light at the corner behind me, timing the period I was alone as the ticking of a clock would have. The only other sound was of the automobiles as they started after the light changed.

Two college boys came out of a boarding house up the street, in the direction I was facing, and passed me. An old man walked by slowly, going the other way. The traffic light clicked on and off. Mr. Dickinson came out of the restaurant and looked in the automobile window.

"Won't you come in and eat now?"

"I don't want anything."

"Do you want me to send you out a sandwich, if you don't want to come inside?"

"No, thank you. I'm not hungry."

And it really seemed to me that I was not. What was hunger, anyway? It was a desire so much easier to control than the other I felt. I had the strength to make up my mind not to eat, but I did not have the strength to resist withdrawing into myself when I was caught between impossible alternatives. And, so long as I could choose, maybe hunger was not so unpleasant. I could imagine the taste of the sandwich. The thought of it brought the flavor of the melted butter to my mouth. But it somehow justified the way I had acted and palliated my sense of shame if I proved to myself that I had the will power not to eat. I had not wanted to cause trouble, and I had not been able to prevent what had happened. But at least, I had the self-respect to resist something as merely pleasant as satisfying hunger. My renunciation made me happier. I felt a little less isolated from the others. But when they came back to the automobile, I was still unable to meet their eyes. Cut off from them, I myself seemed all I could cling to. Clinging to myself cut me off from them more. Yet I did not know what else I could do. And we rode in silence through the Sunday twilight toward home.

The Rain

ᄃᄃᄃA summer downpour.

I am sitting on the back porch, watching the rain fall. At the corner the rain pipe is broken, halfway between the porch and the ground six feet below. The rain barrel that used to be there is gone; the water, gushing out, makes a pool; on it bubbles form, then float on little rivers across the back yard toward the oak tree, beneath which my brother and I have built our town —a group of stones and lines scratched in the earth.

I watch as though nothing more interesting will ever happen. Events do not interest me; only objects: marbles, candy boxes, sticks. My nature is like that of a sprout of the kudzu vine growing in the vacant lot. The trailing stems send down roots and make new plants that are in no way separate from the parent ones. Only somewhere deep down in me does individual consciousness stir.

The rain, an object that is also an event, is one of the things to which it responds. No one else is much interested in these downpours, but my awareness is sharpened by them. The familiar yard becomes strange, as though reality may not be as simple as it seems; the barn and the corrugated-tin garage, the trees along the back street, the known weeds and paths are suddenly as unfamiliar as a scene of an African jungle on the screen of the movie house at Tenth Street.

Over my head the tin back-porch roof is thundering under the fall of water—a sound I am familiar with from listening to the rain's comfortable rumble as I lie in bed at night with my eyes closed waiting for sleep. Even in the dark this visible change must occur. Not only in the back yard but in the whole neighborhood, the whole world that I know, everything must change as it is changing now.

The sidewalk is deserted for the length of the double block in which we live. Only automobiles pass; and streetcars, spraying water from the inundated tracks. The green shingle house beyond the McCrareys' has deepened in color, the way the green leaves of the trees in the back yard have deepened; and, farther on, the raindrops are making bubbles and rings all over the gray surface of the deserted Woman's Club pool.

Everywhere, the impossible is happening: two things, the rain and the landscape, are occupying the same space at the same time.

By the hedge separating the green shingle house from the Woman's Club, a walk, splattered with wet acorns and oak leaves, runs all the way back to the pool. When the sun shines, the pool, painted white and aquamarine, is full of clear water through which the light falls all the way to the blue bottom and reflects back onto the shouting and splashing bathers and the sunburned and peeled body of my cousin, Carl, the lifeguard.

A cement area surrounds the pool, enclosed by a wooden lattice at the back. Through this lattice one can look down to Crescent Avenue. And on the side toward the building, cement steps descend to the basement dressing rooms, beneath the stage of the Club's auditorium. The basement floor is covered with wooden slats (like sections of the lattice laid on its side) through which water drips from my bathing suit and wet feet as I go down to dress after swimming. Wooden walls separate the dressing rooms into individual compartments, but as I dress I hear the voices of the older boys and girls, an echo ringing over their words, like the echo of chlorine hanging over the odor of damp concrete.

Now there are no voices at all, and no one, except the Negro janitor looking out the basement door at the gray pool.

Beyond the Woman's Club, a group of stores runs to the corner; there (for this is as far in this direction as I ever go) my imagination turns down the long, sloping, tree-shaded block toward Piedmont Park. On this street a boy, soaked through his shirt and trousers to the skin and no longer having any reason to hurry, walks slowly homeward. At the park end, a Confederate soldier, kneeling with lowered gun, and the Goddess of Peace, extending an olive branch above him, stand motionless in the rain. Mother, in a long white dress, when she was sixteen, was present at the ceremony of their dedication, and the sight of them always reminds me of the thick black pages of her photograph album.

Beyond the Peace Monument, the level of the park drops to
a large, oval, and completely deserted playing field, from which
a number of ballplayers have fled a short time since, and then
drops again to a clayey, shady stretch where there is a bandstand,
not used for music but for picnics, and where little rivers of red
water are running across the clay in the same way the little rivers
of clear water are running across the back yard now.

Here Mother's whole family—my aunts, uncles, cousins—
sometimes gathers for picnics: fried chicken, tuna-fish sandwiches, potato salad, olives, dill pickles, buttered rolls, jugs of
tea, and a watermelon kept cold in the tub with the ice for the
tea. Afterward we play a game of charades, divided into two
teams, in turn skipping toward each other and chanting:

> "Rum-tum-tum, here we come."
> "What's your trade?"
> "Sweet lemonade."
> "How do you spell it? . . ."

Across the drive from the picnic grounds is the bathhouse and
lunch stand, into which all the players from the game field
crowd in a rain like this, when the shelter of the trees is not
enough to keep them from getting soaked. Beyond the bathhouse is the cement children's pool, also deserted, and beyond
the pool the deserted lake, with the wooden diving tower. The
empty lifeguard's boat is moored beside the boardwalk that sep-
arates the two.

If this were another year, Uncle Herbert would be lifeguard
for Piedmont Park and I would have a job, for a dollar a week,
taking his supper to him from the house on Twelfth Street,

where it is prepared by Mrs. Akin, Mother's second cousin, who insists on my calling her "Aunt Florence," and whose hair is dyed solid blue black, pulled back straight from her forehead and knotted in a large bun on the nape of her neck.

The supper is hot, with a napkin tied around it, holding in the heat but letting out enough of the odor for my walk—down the steep hill of Twelfth Street into the park and along the magnolia-lined path circling the fishing lake—to be accompanied by the fragrance of cooked meat, sweet potatoes, biscuits, greens boiled for hours with large hunks of salt pork. Through the napkin I feel the hot circular base of the plate on the palms of my hands as I carefully balance it upright. In my side pocket I carry the thermos jug of hot coffee. My uncle eats late, at seven-thirty or eight o'clock, and I make the trip after my own supper. But even when I return, after having delivered the meal to him in his rowboat, the light is just beginning to fade, in the summer dusk, to a darkness equalling that of the rain now, and under the magnolia trees around the lake the first couples are just beginning to arrive, in the swings that circle the top of the bank, between the walk and the water.

Passing among the heavy trees and shrubs of the park, I do not *think* of them, any more than now I *think* of the rain. I am not separate enough from the moisture, the grass, and the leaves. At our house, in the spring, I am aware of the blossoming of the apple trees and the pear tree; but in the park I hardly distinguish one tree from another. I take no interest in the various blossoms and seed fruits. As I walk between them and the gravel and water, I do not think of anything. But I am calmed by their presence as I am calmed, to a greater degree, by this precipitation of moisture. I feel in a quiet and latent form the emotions from which thought springs.

The summer my uncle is lifeguard I go away, as other summers, to visit Aunt Winnie; and while I am gone the job of taking the hot supper from Mrs. Akin's house to the park falls to a red-headed cousin of mine, a year older than I am. When I return, my cousin does not want to give up the job. The Monday I am to take over, he arrives in the kitchen on Twelfth Street at the same time I do. Mrs. Akin sends him away. The job has been promised to me, she reminds him; that was the condition on which he took it while I was away. And he must be a gentleman.

I come back from the park, up the same block, and return the empty thermos jug and plate. Between Mrs. Akin's and home, above the cobblestone alley that runs from Twelfth to Thirteenth Street (where my cousin lives) and behind the Gulf filling station, there is a high stone wall along the edge of the sidewalk. On top of the wall the hedge still grows that enclosed the yard of a house that was torn down to make room for the filling station. As I walk beside the wall there is a rustling in the hedge.

"Hey!"

My cousin drops on me. I am knocked off balance; my shirt tears. He draws back his fist to take aim and mutters through clenched teeth in a tongue-tied voice:

"I'll teath you to take my job."

I jerk away. The two of us fall to the sidewalk together, rolling in the dirt that blows down from the hedge. My cousin is tougher than I am; he knows how to fight. But I make up in resentment what I lack in experience. In a few minutes I am running up the block and across the street toward home, sticks and leaves in my hair, my trousers dirty, my shirt torn, my eyes streaming; and in my knuckles almost as much sensation of the blows I have given as in my scratched cheek and cut lip of the ones I have received.

But this day in the rain, the park is only the playing field and, near Tenth Street, a red clay bank that I once climbed up and was afraid to climb down. Farther along on Tenth Street is the grammar school I attend, closed for the summer, the empty windows looking out onto the wet gravel yard, above which, a few minutes ago, as above the woodpile in front of me, flashes of lightning turned the air pale violet, while the odor of ozone descended from nowhere. The white cement pavement of this street slopes so steeply down from the movie theatre, past the school and all the way to the park, that the water cascades into the sewers on the corners with a sound as loud as the roar above me now on the tin roof. This is the block I take when I walk home from school; it leads me to Peachtree and the shopping district, where even such a downpour as this does not banish all the people under awnings and in doorways, and where there are two five-and-ten-cents stores, one directly across the street from the other—Kress's and Woolworth's.

The objects in these five-and-ten-cents stores are displayed on rectangular counters completely surrounding the long narrow alleys where, all day long, the salesgirls stand—small metal auto-

mobiles and tops, rubber balls and metal jacks, boxes of crayons
and water colors, coloring books and puzzles in which metal
shots must be rolled into the middle of a labyrinth. The aisles
are carpeted now, as they are on rainy afternoons when school
is in session, with wet footprints, and give off the odor of black
rubber raincoats.

I go into them whenever I can, but on special occasions I go
into the gift shop, next door to Woolworth's. Turning to it from
the candy, goldfish, and toys of the five-and-ten-cents stores is
turning from childhood to the adult world, the world of art and
culture, and it is there that I go when I want to buy a present
for Mother.

Presents for her are important. I have a great longing not just
to tell her that I love her but to put my love in a physical object
and present it to her. Once in school I made a sugar bowl out
of clay. On the bottom I scratched "To Mother with Love from
Donald." I drew designs on paper with colored crayon, cut them
out, and pasted them on the sides of the bowl after it was hard.
The clay I painted yellow, and over the paint and paper I ap-
plied shellac. The afternoon it was finished I bore it home
proudly. As I hurried up the two granite steps to the front porch,
I fell. The bowl, striking the hard stone, shattered into powdery
fragments, and what a downpour there was from my heart.

The window of the gift shop glows in the rain as though it
were night. If I were there now, I would go inside, look out at
the lights of the automobiles passing in the wet street, and walk
around, followed by the middle-aged woman clerk. There are
candles and glass candlesticks, placemats and finger bowls, china

birds and animals. For Mother's last birthday I chose a single saltcellar (a rabbit, one ear up, one ear down) and a small leather engagement book with a pencil attached to the side.

The rain is lightening; it must be lightening, too, in the block between the shopping district and home, where Blanchard's Funeral Home stands on the corner, an old white clapboard residence. The light inside the Funeral Home is always subdued and gray, as it is outside now. The undertaker has a son a year younger than I am. Once, I went playing with him in the top floor of the house, where the coffins are stored. It was a dark room; I was afraid of the dark; and it should have made a strong impression on me. But it did not. It was not as frightening as our attic, where the ghost Bloody Bones lives. The caskets were as devoid of associations as are the ornamental objects in the gift shop. They might as well have been the gift shop's paperweights of the Statue of Liberty and the White House, which their bronze or silver finish made them resemble. They were objects associated with the events and dramas of life. These surround me as thickly as the galloping red Indians surround the circle of covered wagons on the screen of the movie house on Saturdays; but for that very reason my awareness shuts them out, banishes them, and clings to such peaceful objects as the corrugated-tin garage before me in the rain.

Across Twelfth Street (its red brick pavement glistening in the rain) is Harper's Colonial Florist. A deliveryman hurries a spray of flowers out to the truck at the curb. Mrs. Harper is inside, with her young woman assistant. When I visit them they allow me to go into the back room, behind the great glass-fronted refrigerator full of flowers, which faces out into the shop, and help them wire the stems of galax leaves to the small tooth-pick-like sticks by which they are stuck into the moss-filled frames of the wreaths and sprays. This room, heavy with the moist perfume of flowers and leaves, seems a different world from that of home, but for me it is somehow the same. The women treat me as my mother does; they demand no other efforts, no other responses, than the ones she demands. And there is a fascination, like the fascination in Mother's hairpins and buttons, in these objects out of which floral displays are made—these wires and sticks, and the task of putting them together. The work is so simple that I can do it, yet it is an essential part of the constructing of the ornamental sprays and wreaths, which will be more spectacular but less interesting when they are covered with flowers.

Around the corner of the corrugated-tin garage now, as I sit looking at it, Mr. Peacock appears. He lives diagonally across the street, on the corner of Thirteenth, in an old red brick residence which is the Peacock School for Boys. Mother has given him permission to grow dahlias in our side yard, and at odd hours every day he can be seen from the kitchen and dining-room windows, plodding among the flowers, a thin, gaunt man dressed in old clothes but always wearing his suit coat, collar, and necktie.

"There goes that crazy old Mr. Peacock," my mother or my aunt will say.

He is watering the flowers now, a task which he does only in the rain. Over each of the bushes, planted in rows like corn, he has inverted a cone-shaped vegetable crate to protect the leaves and blossoms. Around each bush there is a shallow ditch to hold water, and moving along now, in the light rain, he is pouring buckets of water beneath certain ones. He has brought his black umbrella, but has attached it to a stick over a plant that has no crate; he himself, without protection from the wet, walks along, leaning to one side under the weight of the bucket of water.

Certain jobs—digging around the plants, cutting them, taking out the tubers to store for next year, and I do not know what else—he does by moonlight; and as he passes the kitchen window at my brother's and my bedtime and sees us being given yeast cakes dissolved in water as a tonic, he scoffs:

"It'd do 'em more good to let 'em come out here with me and open their mouths for the moon to shine in!"

And perhaps he does not mean this wholly as an example of pointlessness, as the family assumes.

But all of his actions are as meaningless to us as storms at sea reported in the newspapers, as the actions of all people who are not members of the family, even though they happen to be in our very yard. He leans over painfully to lift one of the crates and loosen the soil under it a little, then he straightens up, only to lift another and cut a blossom, which glows, lemon-colored or red purple, in the increasing moist light. But it is the quality of the light—violet black in some places, slate gray in others—rather than his actions, that holds my attention.

The light continues to hold me as the sun comes out and illuminates the drops that fall separately from the eaves of the back-porch roof and the leaves of the trees. The world that has been transformed, held in a spell under the advance of the rain, which enters without permission and conjures at its own will, is gradually released. Windows bang up, voices call out. A group of children run from a small frame house into the back street. Upstairs, my aunt coughs. In the side yard, Mr. Peacock takes out his handkerchief and loudly blows his nose.

I go down the steps. At the corner of the house, beneath the broken rain pipe and around the open terra-cotta joint, the water has formed a white throat of sand with a lavalier of pebbles on it, as though to this inland world of hills and houses, pavements and stores, it had brought and gently deposited a memory of the shore of the sea.

Gentian

⊂⊋⊂⊋⊂⊋Between the back porch and the chicken yard of Aunt Winnie's house in Gentian, there stood a chinaberry tree. I do not think that I played under it more than elsewhere. But when my brother and I returned from our visit each summer, it was about this chinaberry tree that I thought, more than about Aunt Winnie and Uncle Emmett and the events of the summer. In Mother's family I had experienced many aunts and uncles. And events happened all the time. But this was the first chinaberry tree that I had seen. For me, the small pointed leaves and the green cherry-shaped berries existed only on that one plant, or beneath it on the blackened wood of the boards on two sawhorses that formed a workbench, and on the tarpaper roof of the brooding house, through whose dusty glass windows I could peer and see the baby chickens swarming in the electric brooder inside. A fig tree grew up through the chicken-yard fence a little farther on. The figs were ripe during our visits. I ate them, and it would have been reasonable if I had remembered the fig tree best, or the pecan trees in the front yard. Nevertheless, I forgot these. We had a fig tree at home, and I had often eaten pecans. But the chinaberry tree and its fruit, eaten by neither animals nor men, remained in my mind. And in the middle of winter when I remembered the summer, I would picture the lean branches and the hard green berries, some of which shrivelled and dried up on the tree, others of which dropped to the ground and lay there, ignored even by the birds, until the flesh over their large seeds grew brown and soft like rotten apples, and almost as unpleasant to step on if you were barefooted as were the droppings in the chicken yard.

Aunt Winnie's house, covered in dark shingles and with a large evergreen camphor bush at either end of the front porch, was like a house in a suburb. And despite the fact that all the surrounding country was farm country, the life lived in the house was not farm life. Uncle Emmett went each morning into Columbus, where he worked as superintendent of a textile mill. My three cousins, all older than my brother and I, each went to college and took jobs away from home. But everything about the house tended by my aunt—the sword ferns and geraniums, the maidenhair ferns and forget-me-nots, lining the front porch in lard cans and flowerpots and boxes, and the animals and chickens in the back yard—was as luxuriously rural as those on the surrounding farms.

The food was rural, too, especially in its abundance, and during the last week of our visit, when Mother always came down from Atlanta to join us, every meal was like Sunday dinner. We ate fried chicken twice a day, for dinner and supper, and Aunt

Winnie, who raised broilers and fryers, gave me my favorite piece, the brain, which I had learned to like from my Donaldson grandmother but no longer got in the city, where store-bought chickens were headless. Aunt Winnie cooked it the way my grandmother had cooked it—inside the skull—and I cracked the skull the way my grandmother had taught me, by rapping it on the edge of my plate. It broke open, like an English walnut, and the brain, about the size of a large nut meat, came out. Or if it did not, I sucked it out, and although I particularly liked the taste, I am not sure that it was not the complication of getting to it that delighted me most.

The way the evenings were passed was rural, too. Even after Mother came down, there was no entertaining or visiting at Aunt Winnie's. After supper, we sat out beneath one of the two pecan trees in the front yard and watched the sky—so much more brilliant than it ever was in the city—for late-summer showers of falling stars. Uncle Emmett pointed out the Big and Little Dippers, and Venus and Mars, as he smoked his cigar and blew heavy clouds of smoke around us to keep away the mosquitoes. If this did not work, Aunt Winnie burned a bit of rag soaked in kerosene, and the odors of cigar smoke and burning flannel competed as we sat in the dark, talking, listening to the crickets, and watching the sky. Sometimes the conversation touched on my father. We had no contact with any other member of his family except Aunt Winnie, and perhaps it was odd that we were so close to her. But she had been close to my father when they were children, and she was particularly fond of my brother, in whom she saw a strong resemblance to him. My father had disappeared from her life as well as from ours. It was only very occasionally that she had word of him. Silences, more than news, expressed the bond between us; and even when he was mentioned, the conversation usually slipped on to other subjects long before the mosquitoes drove us inside to watch Uncle Emmett twist the dials of his short-wave radio, on which he sometimes picked up broadcasts from England, France, or Germany, or to go upstairs to the big, screened sleeping porch and to bed.

Each day, I spent a good deal of time rolling an automobile tire, either with my brother or by myself. I liked wandering about the yard and the surrounding fields. I was never lonely when I was by myself, only when I was around people of whose affection I was unsure, and in the country rolling an automobile tire had the happy advantage of carrying me alone all through the yard and the surrounding hot, dusty, weed-choked landscape. Each day, I started out from the back yard, where the tire usually lay in the place I had left it the evening before, somewhere beyond the well and near a shed that was full of rusted motor cases and other discarded parts of old automobiles. First I rolled the tire along the smooth earth of the driveway, which left the road and went around the house and came back to the road, making a horseshoe. In my imagination the tire was a vehicle, and when I had driven it to all parts of the yard I would make a long-distance trip, between the rows of the plowed field of cornstalks on the other side of the dirt road, or through the plum orchard and up past the house of an old lady who had been my father's and Aunt Winnie's schoolteacher when they were children, and down the slope on the far side of her house to the creek. With my brother and the youngest of my three cousins I sometimes went swimming there, but it never occurred to me to go swimming alone, and when I reached that far by myself I rolled the tire back to the house and played in the yard or beneath the chinaberry tree.

It was the chinaberry tree, the yard, and the tire that I thought about, but none of these was the important thing in my summers; it was Aunt Winnie. Never having known my father or any other member of his family except her well enough to guess what they were like, I had only her to turn to for traits resembling my own which might have been his or theirs. Aunt Winnie was unique, the way the chinaberry tree seemed to be. But it was through the yard around the chinaberry tree, particularly the chicken yard, that I made contact with her, and even there my interest, I would have said, was not in her but in the eggs. My passion for gathering them was as great as that for rolling the automobile tire, and not even the unpleasantness of the chicken droppings squishing up between my toes was sufficient deterrent against the joy of looking into nests and finding eggs, oval and perfect, lying in the midst of their straw-lined emptiness. I was afraid of the chickens—as I was of cows and horses—and I would not put my hands into the nests that had hens on them, as Aunt Winnie did, and take the eggs out from beneath the hen. But my pleasure in the search overcame my fear. Of all the other entertainments I knew, I enjoyed most the magic shows I was taken to at the Sunday school building of All Saints' Church in Atlanta, and I longed to be a magician. But looking

into each of the crates nailed on the back and side walls of the
three-room chicken house and finding the previously empty
nests with eggs in them was far more absorbing to me than
watching a magician pull a rabbit out of a top hat. My dis-
appointment when a nest was empty, or my joy when it contained eggs, was as close as I came to facing the mystery of my
dependence on a world beyond my influence or understanding,
and today when I look into the mailbox and find that it is empty
or that it contains a longed-for letter, the emotions I feel are
echoes of the ones I felt then.

Before I went into the chicken yard, Aunt Winnie gave me
a large earthenware mixing bowl to gather the eggs in, and when
I had been through the chicken house and looked for hidden
nests in the grass around the edge of the yard, I took the eggs
back to her in the kitchen. She sold eggs as well as fryers and
broilers, and if she was ready to make a delivery when I came
in from the chicken yard, I sometimes rode with her in her old
car. Uncle Emmett bought a new automobile every few years,
switching from make to make and endlessly debating their various merits. But Aunt Winnie never abandoned her old square
Essex. Day after day, summer after summer, she drove it carefully to the end of the driveway, came to a full stop, looked in
both directions, then turned into the dirt road and down to the
highway, where she turned once again and drove into town,
straddling the white line down the center of the pavement at
a steady fifteen miles an hour. Her speed never varied. She only
allowed other cars to pass, swerving over to the side of the
road at the same steady pace, after they had honked several

times, and as they passed she did not glance in their direction
but looked straight ahead, her flower-blue eyes as clear as a
sailor's, her weathered face as determined, and her thin lips,
incurved over her false teeth, as impassive.

This quiet, independent pursuit of her own way was her
most characteristic trait, and even her most happy and out-
going expressions were shaded by reserve. When she kissed my
mother, my brother, and me on our arrival, she did it as shyly
and quickly as a young girl, and that was the last time she kissed
us until just before we left. Her reserve and independence were
present, too, in the midst of the bounty of the meals she
cooked. After having loaded the table with platters of fried
chicken and hot biscuits and vegetables from the garden, she
liked to serve us and not set a place for herself. When Mother
was present this withdrawal in spirit caused too much protest,
so she sat down like everyone else, but to a plate on which she
took only a single biscuit or piece of corn bread, a wing or a
back, and a spoonful of black-eyed peas or beans. Mother accepted Aunt Winnie's explanation that she tasted things in
the kitchen and was not hungry; it was a commonplace that
cooking spoils the appetite. But even then I felt that this was
not the whole reason, and I recognized—with my emotions if
not with my thoughts—that turning aside of the will which,
finding insufficient outlet, or not the outlet it wants, is forced
to exert itself at last in renunciation, especially in a renunciation
of what it has itself prepared, and a renunciation no one else
can protest or rightfully take offense at.

Her blue eyes and her girl-like kisses were the only clues I had to my aunt's youth. The facts I learned about her and my father's childhood were as sparse and as bare as the south Georgia country was in those years. I was told, when I asked about Aunt Winnie's name, that my grandfather, who was a cabinetmaker and furniture finisher, had been working at the Winnie Joe Willingham Lumber Company in Tennessee when she was born and had named her after it. And I knew that as children they had lived first in Columbus, where my grandfather had owned a house, and that later the whole family had moved to the country. During the years I visited Gentian, my grandfather was still alive—a poor man, and living in Columbus—but he had married again after my grandmother's death, a woman with five children, and Aunt Winnie, who disapproved of the marriage, did not speak to him. I never saw him during our visits, and her disapproving character hid most of the rest of the past of the family as well. She and my father had graduated from St. Elmo Academy, although the other four children in the family had gone to the public schools in Columbus, and there was a photograph in Aunt Winnie's bedroom of her taken at her graduation or on her wedding day soon afterward. But I knew nothing of how the flowerlike schoolgirl I saw in the picture had grown into the quiet and weathered countrywoman I visited, and nothing of what her hopes and disappointments had been, but only the energy they had given her.

Uncle Emmett was far more expansive and easy-going, and plump and talkative. In my experience, their marriage was a happy one. Their house was pleasant to visit in, which often was not true of the houses of my uncles and aunts on Mother's side of the family. Still, because I stayed with Aunt Winnie and Uncle Emmett for such long periods of time, I saw some of the friction that is inevitable between people who have lived together and shared each other's existences for twenty years, and there were occasions when I glimpsed beneath the surface of Aunt Winnie's character. One night, after she and Uncle Emmett had crossed each other about something, I saw her withdraw physically as well as spiritually, walk out of the house, no one knew where, perhaps into the chicken yard or the cow pasture or one of the gardens—somewhere, I believe, where she could see and hear what was going on, but in any case somewhere where she could not be found—and she did not appear again until the next morning, when she was moving about at her usual early hour in the kitchen. Her face was impassive, her work shielding her thoughts as she prepared breakfast for my uncle and my three cousins, my brother and me, the cats and dogs and chickens, then drew water from the well, brought in Mason jars from the garage, and scalded them so they were ready to fill from the big kettles on the stove, where she was already cooking the fig preserves, blackberry shrub, tomato chowchow, pickled peaches, or whatever it was she was preserving that morning. She did not put her thoughts into words. Work provided the outlet for her feelings. And on that occasion as on others, whatever more I saw of her sadness or her joy, beyond what was apparent in the weathered passivity of her face, I saw transformed into the food she prepared, the tablecloths she crocheted, the pot holders she sewed, the wall

plaques she made from the tops of cigar boxes, the topiary
roosters, baskets, and balls she clipped from the privet hedges
in the flower garden. Some of these handicrafts were based
on instructions in the pages of *Popular Mechanics* or *Farm &
Fireside*, and many of them sold at the Muscogee County Fair,
but all of them, even those which were wholly her own, seemed
strangely impersonal in comparison with the intensity of her
will, which I had glimpsed, and her likes and dislikes, her loy-
alties and withdrawals.

It is quite possible that Aunt Winnie cared less for all these
things she made than she did for the furniture and the other
store-bought possessions about the house that resembled those
I knew at home but that were made unimpressive in my eyes
by the very same country associations that added to the interest
of the others—the strange odors of camphor in the bedrooms,
of hard-water soap at the faucet on the back porch, and of the
outhouse as you approached it through the weeds at the end
of the yard. It did not occur to me that she might care most
of all for the money her work brought her and for the independence of using it to make her home, and her and her children's lives, into something more like the city life I knew. But
wherever the importance lay, she labored over her work with
persistent and solitary devotion, and it is impossible not to
imagine her feelings the day she was home alone and the house
caught fire. Sparks falling from the chimney ignited the roof;
in no time at all, the building was a roaring inferno. The only
things that she and the neighbors who came to her aid were

able to save were a few blistered pieces of furniture from the living room and dining room. The house burned to the ground with everything else in it. In a matter of hours, she was not only homeless but bereft of the slowly accumulated results of her life work, and faced with the equally hard alternatives of a despair as great as her loss and a courage strong enough to go on.

My brother and I did not make our visit that year. But the next summer, when we came down, Aunt Winnie and Uncle Emmett and their son (both their daughters were married by then) were living on the second floor of the double, corrugated-tin garage that Uncle Emmett had built opposite the chinaberry tree. The weight of the sun that summer lay upon the tin building and the yard and the surrounding Chattahoochee river-bed country like the weight of homelessness itself. Each day, the heat fell unbroken over the burned foundation and over the bare driveway and the yard full of wooden frames in which Uncle Emmett and a helper were making white cement bricks. It was too hot to roll an automobile tire, too hot to do anything but go for a swim in the creek, and we went there with our cousin in the afternoons. But in the early mornings, when we got up to join Uncle Emmett in the yard and watch him supervise the pouring of the bricks before he went to the mill, Aunt Winnie was already up and working, having by then calmly accepted what had happened as the continuation of what she knew life to be, and she was still at her tasks when we joined Uncle Emmett again in the evenings, after he came home from work, and helped to empty the white bricks from the frames and add them to the piles stacked at the side of the levelled and cleared foundation.

The new, flat-roofed house was visible from the highway as my brother and I arrived the following summer, driven down by one of Mother's sisters and her husband. At a distance, it possessed an institutional, prisonlike look. And after we had turned up the dirt road to the house and parked the car beneath the chinaberry tree in the back yard and gone inside, our highway impression was corroborated. No part of the house was made of a material that would burn. The floors were of poured concrete, the door and window frames of metal. There were bathrooms and running water, and there was a screened porch opening off the driveway porte-cochere, as there had been in the old house. But there was none of the small, shaded, and gardenlike quality I remembered. There was no sleeping porch, either, and the kitchen no longer seemed, as it once had, a more wonderful part of the back yard. All resemblance to the house on whose foundation it was built was missing, just as sometimes in a woman all resemblance to the girl she was will be lost. But if Aunt Winnie regretted the change she did not say so. She had flowers blooming again in boxes and cans on the porch. And she was busy making new tablecloths, new aprons, and new pot holders, and selling more chickens, more eggs, and more butter than ever before.

Aunt Winnie's predilections were no more concealed than her dislikes. I was fully aware that she preferred my brother to me. This did not make me jealous; but the summer that I was eleven, and we were visiting Aunt Winnie in the old shingle house, which was still standing then, his affection for me was already beginning to be much less than mine for him. And I could not yet bear to be excluded. It did not hurt me that Aunt Winnie took his side one day when we had a fight; I was accustomed, when I had a need for intimacy, to turn to her oldest daughter, Vivian. But that day, when I sought out Vivian, I found her cross with me, too. The comfort I wanted was to be told that I deserved to be loved by my brother and that he was wrong not to love me. And when I was dissatisfied with what she offered instead—permission to paint with the poster colors she used at the school where she was a teacher—she lost her temper. With her classroom sharpness, she told me that I was very bad, and that if I could not behave the way my brother did and be the kind of boy he was, I could not expect him or anyone else to like me.

I do not think she imagined the effect her words would have. I shouted that I did not want her or anyone else to like me, and ran down the steps and out of the house. On the porch, where she caught up with me and tried to stop me, I grabbed a flowerpot and would have thrown it at her if it had not been too heavy. Uncle Emmett, who had been reading the Sunday paper on the side screen porch, came to see what was wrong. I broke loose and ran down the steps, past the pecan trees and across the driveway to the road. Uncle Emmett started after me. He was not angry. He did not know what the upset was about. But he was not used to running, and by the time we reached the top of the hill and passed the house where my father's and Aunt Winnie's old schoolteacher lived, he was out of breath. He lost his temper and his wind at the same time. Stopping in the middle of the road, he shouted for me to come back. But his change of mood was clear in his tone, and I ran even faster, gaining for once that speed I longed for in dreams when I was trying to escape from some terror just behind me. When I reached the bottom of the hill, my uncle was out of sight. He called once more for me to come back. Then he was out of hearing.

No destination was in my mind when I ran across the yard or I would have turned in the direction of the Warm Springs highway at the foot of the hill. But as I slowed down, panting to catch my breath, I remembered that the road I was on joined the Hamilton highway two miles farther on. When I reached there, I decided, I would turn in the direction of Atlanta. There were always automobiles on the highway on Sunday going from city to city, and the idea of having to stop one and ask for a ride the hundred miles to home was less unpleasant than the idea of going back.

I had run away once before. That, too, had been when Mother was not present. She was out of the house for the afternoon, and the trouble was my familiar one with my brother. About five o'clock he came down to the back of the yard where I was playing and told me to come inside. I did not obey at once and he grabbed me and tried to drag me. When he did not succeed he said that it did not matter: I would have to come in sooner or later, and when I did I would get a beating.

I believed most things my brother said, but one thing was not true: I did not have to go back inside if I did not want to. Reluctantly, I made my way down the bank at the back of the yard to Crescent Avenue, and along it to Fourteenth Street. On Fourteenth, I walked out of the neighborhood I knew, past the vacant lot and the Bar-B-Que drive-in at Spring Street, out of the residential district and through the fields and farms and packing houses along Howell Mill Road. I went several miles into the country before my courage failed. It was long after dark when I returned home. But even then it was not from fear that I turned back so much as it was from my discovery that, away from home, there was no place to go.

There was a place to go from Gentian, however. As I walked I thought of that earlier night when I had reached the house, after my suppertime, after my bedtime, even, and Mother had been so relieved and glad to see me that she had not whipped me, but had wept and kissed me and given me something to eat at the large, round, empty dining-room table, already cleared for the night, before she put me to bed.

I was nearly two miles from the house and almost to the Hamilton highway when I heard Aunt Winnie's Essex coming up the middle of the dirt road behind me at its slow, inevitable speed. When she was beside me she stopped, leaving the motor running, and reached across and opened the door. She was alone in the car. Her face was as calm and gentle as ever, her voice as matter-of-fact.

"Get in," she said.

"No."

"You aren't mad with me, are you?"

"No."

"Then get in. I'm going to Miz David's to deliver some eggs and you can ride with me."

I got in. Aunt Winnie started the car.

"You mustn't pay any attention to Vivi," she said. "She's got a temper like her daddy."

She did not ask me what had happened. She knew; or, at least, she knew how to treat someone who felt as I felt.

"I bet I've forgot the butter," she said. "Look on the back seat in the bowl and see if it's there."

I looked. The butter was in the bowl, wrapped in white paper, balanced on top of the eggs.

"You know that your Aunt Winnie loves you, don't you?" she asked me.

"Yes."

"That's good. But do you know what I've done? I've forgotten the milk. People like that Vivi get you so flustered you don't know what you're doing. But you just have to pay them no mind if they hurt your feelings, and go on about your business."

We returned home the long way around, and just before we got to the house, Aunt Winnie stopped at the store at the bottom of the hill, between the Warm Springs highway and the railroad tracks, and bought us each a Nehi soda. From where we stopped we could see Aunt Winnie's house and the "railway station"—a bench at the side of the tracks with a roof over it and the name of the stop on top of the roof.

Between swallows of her soda, Aunt Winnie told me how Gentian had got its name. It had been a long time ago, even before my grandfather had moved nearby. There were no houses and no store, and when the Southern Railway line was built through, the workmen named this obscure stop for the blue flowers they could see growing wild all about them in the woods. The blue flowers had been everywhere, she said, but they were gone now. Driving back to the house, I could see none—only the chinaberry tree.

The Chifforobe

The chifforobe in the living room at home had two large drawers below and two closets above, with mirrors on the inside of the doors, the whole topped by a high ornamental molding. It contained Mother's coats, raincoats, and other outdoor clothes, and my brother's, and mine. For a while it also contained, on the floor of one of the closets, proof of Mother's financial innocence and optimism. Faced with the need of money, she had answered an advertisement in a magazine, which said that a good extra income could be made at home by painting hand-decorated handkerchiefs. She had sent away for the paints and silks, and had filled in some of the stamped flower designs on the silks before she was brought to a halt by the knowledge—which should have been apparent from the arrival of the C.O.D. package of bottles and silks, but which she had avoided as long as she could—that the handkerchiefs had to be sold by the person who bought the materials. She wrote to the company that had sent them to her and asked if they did not want to buy the finished handkerchiefs. Her impression when she answered the advertisement had been that they would, and she was sure that they were more likely than she was to be in touch with people who would want them. There was, of course, no answer, and Mother never finished the remaining handkerchiefs. But she did not feel that she could throw away the materials, which had cost several dollars at a time when dollars were increasingly scarce, and the small cardboard box containing the bottles of aniline dyes remained sitting on the floor of the closet on the left side of the chifforobe for a long time—a reminder of the treachery of the business world.

Mother's innocence was understandable. Her father had been certain that there would be no reason for a daughter of his to work. His certainty had seemed justified; it was his boast that he owned enough real estate in Atlanta to leave each of his nine children a valuable piece of property as well as the income from money he had invested in bonds. Besides, his wife, at the death of her father, a few years before, had been left a third of Mr. Smith's half-a-million-dollar estate. (Mostly property, also.) This and what my grandfather left were joined in my grandmother's estate when she died, the year Mother returned home to live. During the next half decade, Mother did not think much about money. Together with the rest of her brothers and sisters, she received periodic sums of five hundred or a thousand dollars from the estate, and there did not seem to be any reason for the sums to stop. Then the depression arrived. The general disaster of the stock-market crash was followed by a personal disaster for the family. The banker who had handled the investments for the estate committed suicide, and the family discovered that the money they had thought he was investing in Coca-Cola Company stock he had been putting instead, without their knowledge, into a Coral Gables land-development scheme of his own. Only their real estate in Atlanta remained, and its value steadily dropped. The sums of money decreased. Mother, as well as others of her brothers and sisters, had a piece of property deeded to her as a part of her share of the estate. It brought in a small, steady rent. But, needing more money, she put a loan on it; it was lost for the loan; and her already diminished income became even smaller.

Aunt Berta was more realistic and responsible than Mother, with the slightly sharp rightness and exasperation of an eldest sister; and under her guidance, as their incomes dwindled, she and Mother tried various measures of economy. The greatest of these was to give up ordering meat from Knight's Meat Market, where my grandmother had always traded. They were afraid of any change—especially any change that they themselves initiated—and it was a memorable day when they decided to transfer their business to the meat department of the chain grocery store down the street. The orders were still placed by telephone, but the store did not deliver, and now, instead of seeing the truck from Knight's Meat Market at Tenth Street drive into the back yard and the Negro delivery boy hop out and carry the white paper parcel up the back steps to the kitchen door, I would walk down to the corner and pick up a package wrapped in tan paper.

The bills that came at the end of the month were a good deal less, but they were still disconcertingly high. Lily Mae was reprimanded for the amount of food she used in preparing meals, and, between themselves, Mother and Aunt Berta questioned how it was possible for her to take as much food home with her in one little sack as she seemed to. There was no question of letting her go, however; she was the niece of the cook who had worked for their mother, and it would have been as unthinkable to them to fire her as to disown a relative. Still, something had to be done, and Mother and Aunt Berta, not being inventive, decided to do what all the world was doing. One night, over an economical supper of calves' brains and scrambled eggs, my aunt said:

"We'll have to rent a room. With all this empty space, whatever we get will be pure profit."

Aunt Berta put an advertisement in the newspaper. A woman answered it. Her impoverished state made Mother and my aunt exchange immediate glances of dismay. But she was respectable, for they recognized her name as the name of an old Atlanta family that had lost all its money. She paid a week's rent in advance and was given one of the unused upstairs bedrooms.

Our roomer was in her fifties. She did not work, but she was busy. Once or twice a day, she caught the streetcar downtown and returned with small packages and bundles. She had no friends and apparently was alone in the world. But from the number of her errands she seemed to be taking on herself all the arrangements of a large family wedding.

Her taste in clothes was as bright as her life was drab. One day she stopped Mother in the hall, opened the bag she was carrying, and, displaying a piece of gaudy red-and-black printed cotton, said:

"Isn't it lovely?"

"Lovely," Mother agreed.

She escaped, with her mind full of conjectures. Our roomer might have been sewing for herself or for others, but the piece of material Mother had seen was too small for a dress, too small even for a shirtwaist; and, anyway, clothes would not account for the bundle of imitation leather that my aunt had scented out one day when she was supervising Lily Mae's cleaning of the rented room.

Our roomer was not secretive, however. The truth was soon out. It was dolls. Cloth and imitation-leather dolls, with heads at either end, faces on either side of the heads, and a single skirt in the middle, which could hang in either direction. Her trips downtown were to buy materials, or to sell the finished dolls.

"You should try making them," she told Mother.

Mother demurred. "I don't think I could."

"I can teach you. Look. I'll show you. You just cut out the heads with scissors, two at a time, from a pattern. The eyes are buttons you sew on. Then ... wait a minute." She rummaged eagerly in her handbag.

Mother took the opportunity to say, "Some other time. Right now I—"

"All right, dear. You come up and knock on my door any time you aren't busy."

In the chifforobe there was a pad of rent receipts Mother had bought at the dime store, for our roomer, but after the original advance she paid no rent. The second week, she said she would have the money as soon as she went downtown to the bank. The third week, she brushed the matter aside as an unimportant detail. The doll market was not flourishing, but she met misfortune by making ever grander plans. The trouble, she said, was that the stores did not want to bother with the few dolls she could make; they wanted lots and lots, and she renewed her efforts to enlist Mother, and my aunt, too, in her enterprise.

"I know where I can get enough remnants for all three of us," she confided.

She did not avoid encounters. She knocked on the living-room door on her way in and out of the house, to speak to Mother. But Aunt Berta and her children, whose bedrooms were on the second floor, encountered her more than we did, for her room was at the head of the stairs, next to the two bathrooms, which were built side by side, as they usually were in those days, and my aunt couldn't go to the bathroom or downstairs without encountering her.

"She listens through her door until she hears someone in the hall, and then she comes out," Aunt Berta said. "Then nobody can get away from her. It would be bad enough to have her here for such a little bit of money. It's too much for nothing at all. She has to go."

"But how can we make her go?" Mother asked. "When you told her that she had to pay the rent, she simply said for you not to worry."

She had said the same thing when my aunt pointed out that she was keeping food in her room although she had agreed not to. And she did not avoid further reminders about the rent any more than she avoided encounters. Her excuses seemed wholly negotiable to her, and she began to bring up the subject herself.

"We'll have to tell her that it isn't the rent," my aunt decided, "but that Herbert is coming back home and has to have his room again."

Aunt Berta stood her ground against our roomer's affable insistence that it did not matter what room she had, and against her sudden switch to the offensive, in a threat to exclude Mother and my aunt entirely from her doll business. At last, seeing that she had no alternative, she agreed to go. Mother, as sorry as she felt for her, was glad to see her leave. The whole incident was too close to that of the hand-painted handkerchiefs.

Once more the privacy of the homeplace was inviolate. The whole gamut of Mother's and my aunt's financial ingenuity, however, had been run, and they were back where they had started. There was nothing to do but to make a telephone call to Clark, the administrator of the estate and the one member of the family who had been working regularly all this time, and tell him that they needed money. Uncle Clark was not only the head of the family since my grandparents' deaths, he was the only one of the brothers who had his father's firmness of character, and, like his father, he had established himself in local politics. In my eyes, he possessed Aunt Berta's formidability, but to a much greater degree; and even for Mother and my aunt it was not as casual a matter to call him as it was to call their less businesslike brothers and sisters. Nevertheless, they had no choice. They telephoned him and told him that they needed ready cash. There was no cash, he replied. The property that remained in the estate, as he had explained before, was only eating up money in insurance and taxes. Recently, he had been forced to advance money from his own pocket to pay them. The value of property was continuing to decrease, and there was no reason to believe that things were going to be better any time soon. Ironically enough, it seemed that this last fact was going to save them. There was no use in holding on to the property any longer. My uncle was planning to wind up the salable part of the estate. He had already started. The process would take a few days more, and he could not give them anything until then. But in a week or ten days they should have what was coming to them.

This conversation greatly relieved Mother and Aunt Berta. They did not know exactly what remained of their father's property, but they knew that the estate still owned a third of the LaSalle Hotel, the old Bachelors' Domain, which their mother and her brother and sister, their Uncle Lee and Aunt

Ella, had inherited from Mr. Smith; a piece of downtown property like that was certainly salable, and they put their hopes on it. They did not need to think up new schemes for the future; they needed only to hold on for a few days longer.

But even holding on turned out to require more ingenuity than they had imagined. When the bill came from the chain store, there was no money to pay it, and the chain store would not carry the bill over as the meat market had.

Suddenly Mother and my aunt found themselves in the position of being able to buy meat and groceries only if they paid cash for them, and there was no cash in the house. Lily Mae, who several times had reluctantly taken a week off, still came to work, although we were behind in her salary; but there was very little work for her to do, outside of cleaning, and almost nothing for her to carry home in her sack at the end of the evening. As a makeshift disguised as a treat, the day that the chain-store manager explained the situation to us, we had for a week night supper what, after large Sunday dinners, had always been a Sunday night treat—Parker House rolls, butter, and jelly. The Parker House rolls Aunt Berta made were delicious; the odor of them cooking was mouth-watering, and it was impossible not to think how good a little cold baked ham would be with them.

The next night, we had them with ham. The ham was brought to us in the afternoon by Mother's Uncle Lee, the co-owner of the hotel that was to be sold. He must have heard of Mother's and my aunt's penniless state in his discussions with Uncle Clark about the sale of the hotel, but he did not mention it.

He acted as though his stopping by the house on this day were a coincidence, and his visit purely social. He drove his automobile into the driveway only as far as the corner of the front porch, instead of going all the way into the back yard, as the butcher's truck had in the past when it was delivering meat. He got out and carried the ham up the porch steps to the front door. He made light of his gift; it had become impossible to obtain real country hams in the city, so he had gone down to the country earlier in the week to buy one, and while he was there it had occurred to him that we might like one, too. But his automobile was at the corner of the house only a short while before he came out, backed it from the driveway, and was gone; and to me his visit seemed a variation of the visits that formerly had been made by the butcher's truck to the back yard.

After he had gone, his visit began to seem odd to Mother and my aunt, too. He had not mentioned the sale of their jointly owned property, and the fact that he surely knew more about their financial affairs than they knew and yet had not brought up the subject made them uneasy. They began to feel that he had not acted like his usual self, and that possibly there was going to be some difficulty about the sale. My aunt, in particular, was certain that she had detected a touch of condescension in his attitude, which had not been there before our finances had begun to wane.

"Anyway, it was kind of him to remember us," Mother said.

"Well," Aunt Berta replied, "I guess he can afford to be kind."

She took the ham back to the kitchen and busied herself with skinning it.

Mother went to her bedroom. Her wardrobe trunk, lined with a cloth of bluebirds flitting in the leaves of trees, was there, opened back against the wall and facing out into the room. The trunk had been given her by her mother as a wedding present. She had used it during all the years she had lived with my father. Now, from habit, and because there were not many closets in the house, she continued to keep some of her dresses on hangers in the trunk. On the other side, her jewelry was kept, in the shallow drawer at the top. She opened it and took out an antique necklace that had been a present from her grandmother—the only piece of real jewelry that she still possessed. Until a few months before, the compartment had also contained her diamond brooch and diamond engagement ring. One of her brothers had pawned them for her. She had thought that she would have redeemed them by now. But there was only the necklace. And, despite her fondness for it, it was not worth much.

The night after the ham was gone, Uncle Smith and Herbert came by the house on their way home from a hunting trip in the south of Georgia. Dressed in khaki shooting jackets and pants, with bags of quail, doves, and rabbits hanging from their waists and the cold air and fresh odors of outdoors still clinging to them, they appeared at their best on visits like this. Red-cheeked and smiling, they went straight to the kitchen and gave Mother and my aunt enough birds and rabbits for a large meal. Then they came back up the hall with their sisters, pausing and talking in loud voices about their trip. Just before they reached the front door, Mother drew Uncle Herbert aside and told him that she wanted to speak to him privately for a moment in her bedroom.

The next day, he brought her a pawn ticket for her necklace and the three dollars that was left after he had paid the interest on her other jewelry. Instead of putting the ticket in the trunk, where the necklace had been, she placed it with the other pawn tickets in the chifforobe in the living room, on the same side with the cardboard box of aniline dyes and where she kept her pocketbook and "business papers." Beside them was my grandparents' Bible. Mother's father had read it aloud to the family each evening when she was a child; and often, in imitation of him, she had started reading it to my brother and me, a chapter an evening, intending to go all the way through. But, sooner or later, something inevitably interrupted the readings. Our place became lost in Leviticus or Numbers. And when we started again, we went back to the beginning. The Bible had not been out of the chifforobe for the last few months, but the sight of it and the thought of her father gave her a certain comfort. He had started out a poor man after the Civil War, in a world in which people lived on salt pork, corn bread, and syrup, and he had risen to a position of wealth and security in a society where no one ate such rations except Negroes, sharecroppers, and convicts. When he was alive, he could not have conceived of one of his daughters with only three dollars to her name; such predicaments did not come about in a God-fearing and respectable world, and the fact that he could not have pictured her in the present situation helped her to believe that it could not last.

She took the Bible out of the chifforobe and began reading at the first page:

"In the beginning God created the heaven and the earth."

The voice she heard in memory that evening was forceful and authoritative, but the one I heard in the living room was uncertain and faint.

For Mother it was not a long way from thoughts of her father to thoughts of her oldest brother. She decided that it was not possible that he, any more than her father, could really comprehend the situation she was in. At breakfast the next morning, she reminded her sister that it was longer than Clark had said it would be before he talked to them again, and asked her what they should do. Going back to the beginning, as in the case of the Bible, they examined their situation and once more decided, as though it were some entirely new idea that they had not presented to him before, that they would call him and tell him they absolutely had to have some ready cash.

"When do you think would be the best time to telephone?" Aunt Berta asked.

"What about right after breakfast?" Mother suggested.

Their brother's wife answered, which they considered a bad omen, but when he came to the telephone to speak to them he said, to their relief, that he was glad they had called. All the papers were ready. He could not come by the house that day, but he would come tomorrow. It would be as much of a relief to him as it was to them to get everything settled, and he hoped that everyone would be satisfied with what he had arranged.

Mother and Aunt Berta were delighted. Mother did not smile by turning up the corners of her lips; she opened her mouth wide, showing her beautiful, even teeth, and beamed. The difficulties she had been through had not dulled her youth or added the thinnest protecting caution over her optimism. There was something out of place, something awkward and unnatural in expressions of concern on her countenance. She seemed to be "making a face" all the time she was unhappy. I longed to stop her, and it was like having a blemish removed to see her smiling again.

To celebrate, we had steak that night, cooked a long time, smothered in thick milk-and-flour gravy, with Lily Mae's biscuits to sop up the gravy.

"Thus the heavens and the earth were finished," Mother read after supper, when she took the Bible out of the chifforobe again before my brother and I went to bed, "and all the host of them."

It was a cold, dry winter day. Every few minutes, through the living-room window, the trolley cars could be seen showering sparks from the overhead wires as they passed up and down Peachtree Street. Mother had taken the pen and the bottle of ink from the chifforobe and put them out on the living-room table before my uncle arrived, ready to sign whatever he brought. He came in the early afternoon. When Mother and my aunt let him in the front door, he took off his hat but kept on his overcoat. As soon as the three of them were in the living room, the two women simultaneously mentioned the hotel. Their brother stopped and looked at them in surprise. The papers he had brought were not for the sale of the hotel. There had never been any question of selling the hotel. That was the unsalable part of the estate. With real estate prices so far below values, it would be foolish of the co-owners, who did not need money, to even think of selling it. As an example of how low real estate prices were, he did not mind telling them that their mother, the year before she died, had been offered a hundred thousand dollars for the homeplace and had not considered the offer. The best sum that could be obtained for it now was twenty thousand. Nevertheless, with no money in the bank to continue paying insurance and taxes, and no income, the estate had no choice but to sell; and the papers he had brought for their signatures were for the sale of the homeplace. The twenty thousand would be paid as soon as the papers were signed, returned to him, and passed on to the purchasers. His sisters could have their money in a day or two. However, with the price as small as it was, the members of the family who had already been deeded pieces of property would do well to remember that their shares from the sale of the homeplace were apt to be very little.

Uncle Clark was leaving when I came home from school. As he drove his automobile out of the driveway and turned into the street, I stood on the sidewalk, waiting to cut across the drive and over the lawn to the house. He looked straight at me as he passed, and drove on with no sign of recognition. Inside the house, I found Mother and my aunt in the living room, the ink and pen and papers still on the table, the door of the chifforobe swung all the way back, as though it had been forgotten, revealing my brother's overshoes and mine, and Mother's umbrella, on the floor inside.

Mother and Aunt Berta, in an effort at comprehension, were repeating back and forth to each other fragments of the conversation that had just taken place. Their brother had informed them that by the terms of the sale the house would have to be vacated in two months. Faced with the fact that they would soon be as homeless as their recent lodger, they had told him that he would have to help them get jobs. He had replied that, as far as he knew, they had no qualifications for jobs. Then he had gone, leaving the papers on the table, with instructions for the two of them to obtain the signatures of the rest of their brothers and sisters and to return the signed papers to him.

"Why should we get the signatures for him?" my aunt said. "He has an automobile and can go around to everyone and get them himself. And furthermore..."

Mother saw that I was listening. Indicating my presence to her sister, she went to the chifforobe, that solid monument of security out of which she so often had seen her own mother fetch something practical and protecting and matter-of-fact, and took from it her pocketbook. Then she turned to me, held out a coin, and said:

"I want you to go to the store. Here's the money. Tell the butcher that you want a pound—no, two pounds—of salt pork. Hurry, now. It has to be soaked before it's cooked."

Aware that whatever had happened had upset the accepted standards of value, that sparks had fallen from something more than the trolley wires that day, and that Mother, who never concealed anything pleasant from me, was concealing something, I went on my errand.

Later, when the second-hand dealer came to look over the furniture none of the family wanted, I learned that, in his eyes, very few of the pieces were worth much, and that for the chifforobe in the living room he would give nothing at all.

Ruby, Sapphire, Yellow Diamond

CECECEkipping ahead, a last memory of the homeplace. One afternoon, after we had moved away, my brother and I stopped by on our way home from school to see what was happening. Workmen had begun to demolish the house. The roof remained, and the walls were intact, but the door and window frames had been removed. The structure presented a smiling, empty look, like the face of a boy with every other tooth out. It was as open, as airy, as the house we once had put together among the branches of the apple tree in the back yard, over the chicken coop. There was nothing sad in the sight, as there had been in the packing of our possessions before we left. It offered the familiarity of a dream, but no resemblance to the place where we had lived. It looked more beautiful, more carefree, than before, and I was excited to find the removed doors and windows stacked against the tree trunks in the front yard. When the house was built, the street number, 910, was set in colored glass in the fanlight over the front door. Among the leaded panes of glass around the numerals, there were several thick glass brilliants, like those in glass-jeweled belts, only larger. I was delighted by the pools of light they threw on the rug in the front hall when the sun struck them —red, blue, yellow. There was a hatrack in the front hall with a bench seat and arms at either end, and I sometimes climbed onto the arms in an attempt to reach the glass brilliants. I longed to look through them and to see the outside world multiplied by their facets and reduced to the separate colors that they dyed anything, my hand, a piece of paper, a box, that I put in their light on the rug. But even by standing on the arm of the hatrack, I was never able to get near them. Now, here they were, in the fanlight propped on the roots of an oak tree, as available as sticks, and stones, and blades of grass always had been.

My brother said that I should leave the fanlight alone or I would get into trouble. But the workmen were leaving for the day, and when he wandered away, to look at the places where we used to play, I set to work prying loose one jewel of each color. They were not hard to remove. The lead between the panes of glass had already been bent and broken in several places. Soon, I had a ruby, a sapphire, and a yellow diamond, each the size of a fifty cent piece, in my trousers pocket.

I followed my brother into the house. The ground floor rooms, where we had lived, were scattered with house wreckers' tools, like a factory. The floors were covered with dirt and plaster, the walls were bare, and there was a smell of wood and mold that I had never encountered before. Excited, I went up the long, straight staircase to the second floor. Here, the rooms were even lighter and less familiar. Their closets were without doors and their fireplaces without mantels. In some of them, the floor boards had been removed. I mounted the enclosed stairs from the back bedroom to the attic. Afternoon light poured through holes in the walls and roof into this once dark and frightening place. Pretending that I was in a drama like those I had seen on the movie screen, I poked into corners and angles that I had never dared to enter before, and found piles of discarded gas lighting fixtures and the glass-walled safe containing some of my grandfather's tablets and letters.

My brother followed me to the attic. While he was there, I went down to the second floor again. In one of the bedrooms I discovered, piled up together, all of the long, heavy, iron window weights that had been removed from the second story windows. Earlier, when I was looking at the gas lighting fixtures in the attic, one of them had slipped between the cross beams and fallen through the lathing and plaster of the second story ceiling. Now an idea came to me. I picked up one of the heavy window weights and carried it to a part of the room where the floor boards had been removed. Holding it by one end, I threw it up into the air as high as I could. There was a moment of breathless suspense—then the window weight crashed down between the cross beams, through the lathes and plaster, to the ground floor. It bounced on the wood with a loud, echoing sound, and a cloud of dust rose in the air.

I was delighted. It did not occur to me that I was desecrating the house. I was playing a game. Objects were revealing their nature to me, their construction. I took up another window weight, and when my brother came into the room, it was following the first one, crashing through a fresh section of the plaster a short distance away.

He grabbed me and told me that I was a monster, unnaturally devoid of feeling, who did not know right from wrong, and that he would tell Mother what he had seen me doing, if it were not for the fact that, with all her other troubles, it would be more than she could bear.

No sense of having done wrong had prepared me for his words. They fell on me unshielded, a blow that broke the skin of old wounds. I was covered with shame and confusion. But I did not really think that I had done wrong. As I walked home alone, I consoled myself by looking at the world through the red, yellow, and blue brilliants. Something losable, and something unlosable, had been salvaged from the afternoon.

The Glass Doors

⊏⊐⊏⊐⊏⊐Aunt Nettie, the wife of Mother's youngest brother, was secretary to the personnel manager of the Coca-Cola Company. Despite Mother's lack of experience, she got her a job there, as a clerk in the filing department.

By the beginning of March, the homeplace had to be vacated to be torn down. Mother started to work the first week in February. Each day, on her way to and from work, as she looked for a place for us to move, her one criterion was nearness to the house we were leaving. With everything else gone, it would be too much to desert the neighborhood where she had been born and grown up. Also, only by being near could any place we would be able to afford resemble the homeplace.

The rooms she decided on were in a small frame house on Twelfth Street, two blocks away, not far from the house where she was living when I was born. The rent was fifteen dollars a month, and our apartment was dignified by having a separate entrance. Its dignity was humbled, however, by the entrance's opening into what obviously had been, until then, the land-lady's dining room. Behind this, there was a linoleum-floored kitchen, resembling an enclosed back porch, and, upstairs, a bedroom and a bath, both sharing the kitchen's outside, added-to-the-house look.

We carried almost nothing but our clothes with us the first of March when we descended Twelfth Street to the three room apartment. All my grandparents' old furniture was too large to fit into the small rooms. We took, for me and my brother to sleep on, two iron twin beds that had been bought for two of my uncles when they started to college. Aunt Ada, who had recently lost her home, gave us a veneer dressing table and a chest of drawers from her extra bedroom suit. And, on the installment plan, Mother bought a studio couch.

March the first was cold; it was certainly the coldest first of March that fate had ever brought us; and except for the front room, heated by the furnace, none of our part of the frame house was warm. Mother was afraid of the gas burner that heated the bedroom upstairs and did not know how to regulate it. Besides, it removed only the frostiest degrees of the chill. And that first evening, when my brother and I were home from school, and Mother returned from work to cook supper for us, we discovered that in our one warm room there was no privacy.

The landlady's part of the house was connected to ours through double glass doors. The glass doors were curtained and locked from her side, but they could not be locked from ours. This ancient creature, with a broomstick figure and dustmop hair, had only to turn the key in the lock and open the door to stick her head into our living room. This evening, she unlocked the doors while we were sitting down to supper around a card table and gave us instructions on how to adjust the heat register in the floor in order to economize on her fuel bill. Later, Mother saw her peeking from behind the curtains to make sure that her advice was being followed.

This happened three evenings in a row. Despite the cheap rent, Mother began to feel that she was paying to be made unhappy. And in the meantime, only five blocks away, in the nice cream brick apartment house where Aunt Ada lived, an apartment was available, for only a few dollars more a month, in which the worth of those extra dollars would be given us many times over, in comfort and privacy, each month we lived there.

On April Fool's Day, four weeks after we left the homeplace, we moved into the new apartment. Our rent was thirty-two dollars and fifty cents a month. Mother's salary was seventy-five dollars. The situation would have been difficult for anyone, but in Mother's case the difficulty was increased by her inability to believe that the seventy-five dollars a month was all there was. It had never been that way before. Her income, as small as it had become, had always fluctuated and adjusted itself to expenses. Even when it had failed to pay what was owed, there had been an element of chance, a possibility of hope. Now, expenses had to adjust themselves to income. The order of life was reversed as nonsensically as a warning sign read backward in a mirror.

My brother and I worked after school, on alternate shifts as curb boys at Hawk's Drugstore, near Buckhead. Most of what we made found its way to Mother to help pay expenses. But Mother never admitted that we ought to help. It was difficult enough for her not to give us money; she could not face accepting it from us. Each time, our contributions were apologized for and promised to be repaid. From what? From the same nonexistent source that was going to pay the rent, I suppose. I did not understand the impossibility of our finances. It was seeing catastrophes make Mother unhappy that moved me, not the catastrophes themselves. I only understood our poverty when it touched me in some personal way, as it did the day when I had to give up, to pay a bill that was presented at the door, the money I had in my pocket for a haircut. My uncut hair seemed to proclaim to everyone my penniless position, and I refused to go somewhere I had been invited. But, ordinarily, I did not think about money.

My brother thought about it very much. He kept an account of what Mother owed him. He was more aware of her financial affairs than I was, and he thought that they could be straightened out if she would handle them properly. As he made more money than I did, he gave her more, and it angered him to give her money and then to see her use it in ways he did not consider logical. When that happened, he said that she had imposed on him. Many evenings the first year and a half in the apartment on Peachtree Place were spent in arguments about finances. There was a sensible and systematic way to buy what you needed on the amount of money you made, he told her, and he tried to teach her how to budget. Mother listened to him, pretended to see his point and to believe that it was practicable, then went ahead and did what she felt that she had to do. But in one thing she agreed with him: she did not think that she should take his money. Each time she did, she wept and swore that she would never again do it; and each time it was the same. Finally, I was fired from the drugstore for talking back to the manager. For my brother, this was the end. As far as money was concerned, the three of us lived in an armed truce. Mother tried to keep knowledge of her mounting debts from my brother, and I helped her. I really did not know how many debts she had; and in a certain sense, neither did she. She was sure that before they got too bad something would happen. And something did.

The front door of our apartment was made of glass. A tan shade was kept pulled part way down. There was an ecru curtain over it. From the front room, you could look out through the lower half of the door and see who was standing in the hall when the doorbell rang. You saw only legs and feet, but these were usually enough to give you some idea of who was there. I was sure that the dark trousers and shoes I could see belonged to a man I did not know.

I had not made a sound as I crept into the living room to see who was ringing. As silently, I crept out and through the swinging pantry door into the kitchen. The kitchen opened onto a lattice-work back porch from which it was possible to go into the alley that ran along the back of the building. I went out this way, walked around the end of the apartment house, and entered through the front door.

A heavy, official-looking man was standing in front of our apartment, ringing the bell. He glanced at me as I entered, but looked away as I went on up the stairs to Aunt Ada's apartment on the second floor.

"There's a man at our door," I told her as soon as I was inside. "I think he's from the real estate company."

"Hasn't your mother paid the rent?"

"I don't think so."

"I've told her and told her not to get behind."

Aunt Ada was indignant. Indignation gave her energy. She marched out into the hall and called down the stairwell to the man who was ringing our doorbell. She was Mrs. Windham's sister, she said, and demanded to know what he wanted. He was quite willing to say what he wanted. He wanted two months' rent. If it was not paid, Mrs. Windham would be dispossessed and her salary would be garnisheed.

Mother burst into tears when she came home from work that evening and heard what had happened.

"It doesn't do any good to cry, Louise," her sister said.

"But, Ada, what am I to do?"

"You'll have to pay them."

"I don't have the money."

"Doesn't Fred have any?"

"I can't take it from him again. His boy scout troop leaves for Washington this Friday and it will break his heart if he doesn't go. He's been saving up for the trip for nearly a year."

"It won't break his heart any more than being put out on the street, will it?"

"I can't do it."

"Then what can you do?"

"I don't know. I'll think of something."

We were talking in Aunt Ada's apartment. My brother was at the drugstore. Mother made me promise not to tell him what had happened when he came home. Her main concern was to get out of this trouble without letting him discover that she had gotten into it.

That Friday, my brother went to Washington, D.C. with his scout troop. The weekend passed. Monday came and no catastrophe happened. Fred was full of excitement from the things he had seen and done. That evening as he talked about them, it was almost the way things had been in the home-place in the old days.

Wednesday afternoon, when I came home from school, I found the same dark-clothed man in the hall, directing two Negroes in the work of carrying our furniture out of the building. The man was angry. The Negroes were shamefaced. And in the midst of them, everywhere at once, Aunt Ada was more indignant than ever. She had asked to have our possessions carried up to her apartment to save us the embarrassment of seeing them put out on the sidewalk. The man had refused. On the technicality of his having to be legally correct, he insisted on watching each chest and chair, each bed and mattress, removed from the premises of 15 Peachtree Place. He stood halfway up the short flight of marble steps from the entrance to the first floor level, making certain the Negroes took each object out of the apartment, down the half flight to the entrance, and out of the building before they returned and for a promised payment from my aunt carried them up the flight and a half to her apartment.

As I entered, Aunt Ada came into the hall, half a dozen coathangers of clothes thrown across her arm, two pairs of Mother's shoes in her hands.

"Arrest me if you think you can!" she shouted at the man. "But hell will freeze over before you or anybody else alive can stop me from going into my own sister's apartment and taking some of her clothes to my apartment if I want to."

She grabbed hold of my hand and told me to come along with her. Everything was going to be all right. We would stay with her until it was settled where we would live.

All her indignation against Mother was gone in her fury against the man. Even after he and the Negroes left, she remained a torrent of energy, berating him as we stacked our furniture in the front room of her three room apartment, already crowded with possessions from the house she and her husband had lost. Never once, as we made a path through the stacked tables and chests and chairs to set up one of the twin beds and the studio couch, did she admit that there was any difficulty or discomfort, or anything annoying in the whole situation, except the man from the real estate office who had been so contemptible.

Mother came home from work, her eyes red, her cheeks flushed. All afternoon, after Aunt Ada had telephoned and told her what had happened, so she would not be taken by surprise on her return, she had wept when she was alone in the brief privacy of the vault of metal cabinets at the rear of the wire-enclosed filing department. She had tried to keep up appearances when she was where she could be seen by secretaries coming to the department for vouchers and folders. Then she had wept harder than ever when she was alone again, fearing that someone might have noticed her red eyes, that what was happening would be discovered, and that she would be fired. She was ready to lie down and give up. Yet that was even more impossible than keeping on.

My brother had gone from school to work. I watched out of the window of Aunt Ada's bedroom for him to get off the streetcar that would bring him home. Aunt Ada had prepared supper, but no one could eat. Mother was terrified of what would happen when my brother arrived. The worst of his predictions had come true, and her guilt was more than she knew how to excuse. I was as frightened as she was. When I saw him get off the streetcar, I told Aunt Ada. She went down to the entrance of the building to meet him.

When he entered the apartment, Mother was sitting on the twin bed in the crowded living room. Half of all we owned was stacked between them for him to make his way through before he reached her. He sat down beside her, put his arms around her, and wept. As cold as he had been in his disapproval when she ignored his advice, in the face of this disaster his tears flowed like hers. He cried as though his heart was broken, and seeing him cry moved me more than the other events of the day. It had been so long since he had shown either Mother or me anything other than the hard outside of his feelings, that his tears violated everything I had come to feel about him. He said how sorry he was for what had happened, asked why she had not let him know how much rent was due, and promised her that the day would come when she would not have these troubles and he would take care of her. It did not change the situation between us. After his unguarded tears, his respect for money and for the rigid rules of economy became stronger than ever. But Mother felt only that all barriers between them were gone. And I, seeing her consolation in the midst of the disordered furniture, wept with something that was not wholly sorrow.

Uncle Felix came home from his business, and as we sat around the table in the kitchen he gave Mother advice about the best things for her to do the next day. She did more or less what he told her. She took time off on her lunch hour, went to the office of the real estate company, and asked them, please, not to garnishee her salary but to allow her to pay off the back rent, ten dollars a month. Then she inquired for some place for us to live that we could afford. This was a subject that had been discussed before. A housing project was being built near the Coca-Cola Company, a part of the federal government's slum clearance program under Roosevelt, and Aunt Nettie had suggested that Mother should apply for an apartment there. But Mother did not think that the sort of people who would live in a low-income housing project were the sort of people for us to be brought up among. And her brothers and sisters agreed with her. Aunt Ada repeated their opinion that it would be a disgrace for any member of the Donaldson family to live in a public housing project. But Uncle Felix said that they were silly and wrong. Mother should apply for an apartment immediately, and consider herself damned lucky if she got one.

We were to live in Aunt Ada's front room for three months. School would be out and I would be working through the summer for the Atlanta Crackers baseball club in Ponce de Leon Park before we would move into our own apartment again. It was not an easy time for anyone. Many small scenes occurred during our stay which, with the passage of time, have more or less faded from my mind. But I remember the first night clearly. Mother, my brother, and I slept in the disordered living room. Mother was on the studio couch. My brother and I, who had slept apart since we left the homeplace, shared the twin bed. Mother always slept in a nightgown. Sometimes, after she had put it on for the evening, and before she retired, I had seen her kneel on the floor beside the studio couch and say her prayers. That night, I went to sleep long before she went to bed. Toward morning, I awoke. My brother was asleep at my side. But Mother was awake in the middle of the room, visible in the light falling through the glass door from the hall, on her knees between the studio couch and a box of my and my brother's discarded toys, her hands folded in front of her face, her head lowered, her lips moving in the dark.

The Bath Tub—III

Skipping back, a last memory of bathing with my brother. He and I are standing naked beside a white porcelain tub into which steaming water is running from the metal faucet at the end. We are both adolescent. His hair is still straight, the way a young boy's hair is straight; mine is beginning to have a curl in it. The tile-floored bathroom, much smaller than the one in the homeplace, is at the end of the hall in the apartment we are to be dispossessed from on Peachtree Place. To one side of it is the bedroom in which we have left our clothes. Mother is at work at the office. It is after school. I had come home and turned on the water in the tub and was undressing when my brother came in and began to get ready for a bath. For a reason that it does not interest me to discover, he chooses to ignore the fact that I am doing the same thing.

"You can see that I am using the bathroom," I say.

"You can use it later," he answers.

"You can, too."

"But I'm not going to. Go on, get out of here."

"Try and make me."

"I will."

All friendliness between us has disappeared. He gives me a shove in the direction of the door. I hit him. He hits back. This could be one more of the many fights we have had through the years which all end the same. But it is not. The resentment that has been slowly accumulating in me has convinced me for a long time now that he is not going to treat me considerately unless I force him to. This conviction is an extreme one for me. I do not like to force things. I value most what I am given, and value it precisely because it is given. And what I want from my brother can only be given. But it is not going to be given, and I have reached the point where I am willing to abandon hope of friendliness and allow myself to hate him with the hate which is necessary if I am going to fight him with the determination to win. I have been willing to do this for some time; but for anything to come of my willingness it has been necessary for me to have a little of that ingredient without which no one wins in a contest with someone stronger: luck.

And this time I have it. I strike back with all the strength my hate can give me. My blow lands on my brother's chin with a clear, clean crack, like the crack of a dead branch being broken sharply in two. He loses his balance and falls to the floor. His head strikes the tile wall of the bathroom. He does not get up.

And when I have left the room and he does get up, he does not continue the fight. The occasion is unique. It is the first time that I am not the one who loses. And it is the last time that he ever tries to bully me or impose his will upon me by force. There is no tapering off. This is the end. It never happens again.

It is not my triumph, however; friendship was what I wanted, and after this occasion I do not try for it any longer. Where there was once something, now there is nothing. Afterwards, I will feel more strongly than ever that it is those things which I have had and lost, rather than those things which I have never possessed, that create in me the greatest sense of deprivation. But this does not affect events. From this time on, my brother and I have no more to do with each other.

Myopia

ᠭᠭᠭI *am walking up a pavement of hexagonal cement sidewalk tiles. On one side, there are trees that grow in a strip of dirt between the sidewalk and the curb. On the other side, there is a black iron fence around the yard of a Victorian house. The upright spikes of the fence are spears, their fleur-de-lis points at the level of my eyes. The sharp tips make my lids squinch involuntarily, and to avoid them I walk near the trees. Then the sidewalk tilts. I throw my weight on the balls of my feet to hold back, but the fence draws me nearer. The sharp iron points pass so close that the regular succession of their tips is reflected in my eyeballs. My hand raises itself to protect my eyes, but my balance is gone. I am going to fall. My feet are off the ground and I am moving in an arc through the air toward the inverted iron hearts. The spikes flow past so near that all I can see is their upright, black knife blades. In terror, as the points touch my eyes, my lids close. The fence ends, and I fall through*

space to wake with my face on the smooth sheet of the bed I
sleep in.

I had this recurring nightmare regularly in my early adolescence.

Then, one night when I was thirteen or fourteen, I opened a door and saw something that I believe must have been the most upsetting sight possible. It did not consciously upset me at the time. Some shutter in my brain closed before I closed the door. I turned and went back down the hall I had come up, as though I had seen nothing. My mind, by some process I do not understand, swallowed whole, without awareness, what my eyes had seen. Nevertheless, it swallowed it. I can remember now what I saw. I do not know when the sight returned or what called it back. I know only that at the time it vanished, leaving no result that I was conscious of, and that after a long period, when events had separated me from it, the memory came back.

Up until the night I opened the door, I remembered my dreams. Soon after, I ceased to recall them. I still dreamed, but my waking consciousness concealed from itself what sleep revealed. If the recurrent nightmare of the iron fence awoke me, I recognized it. But if any other nightmare broke my sleep, I forgot what it was about by morning. And of all the other dreams I had during the night I remembered nothing.

So long as my dreams had stayed in my consciousness, they had not interested me. After they vanished, I longed to know what I was concealing from myself, and I listened with great interest to the dreams of others. One morning, Mother related, to her horror and my delight, her dream of the night before that she had cooked me and my brother in a large frying pan and eaten us. Did I dream such things? Another time, she told how, after she had gone to sleep, she had found herself at the edge of the sea. In front of her, a narrow plank, no wider than a board in the living-room floor, stretched straight to the horizon. The voice of the Devil told her that she had to walk the plank all the way across the ocean or she would be his, and as she started to walk, she could see endless little blue fiends laughing and grabbing up at her from the sparkling water on either side.

Shortly after I ceased to remember my dreams, I became near-sighted. My self-protecting unawareness apparatus was so efficient that I myself did not discover my inability to see; it had to be pointed out to me. In mathematics class, my last year of junior high school, I was unable to read the equations to be copied down from the blackboard, but I assumed that the hardness of the chalk and the smallness of the teacher's handwriting, not my eyesight, was the trouble. Our seats in class were arranged by our grades, from the front row to the back, and I was always near the back. One day I asked to be allowed to sit at a front desk when there was work to be copied. The teacher gave me permission, but he told me that if I could not see from my regular seat I should go to an eye doctor; I must be nearsighted. I told this to my mother. A visit to an oculist was arranged. The next week, I put on glasses.

My psyche and body did not allow themselves to be fooled so easily. They had more tricks up their sleeve in the effort they had begun toward blindness. With upsetting rapidity, my eyes adjusted themselves. Inside of a year, they saw no more through the concave lenses than they had seen without them, and my glasses had to be made stronger. My mind, too, set to work to shut out my immediate surroundings. I began to read. I do not mean that I read more than before. Until then, I had never read a book for pleasure. That year, I belonged to no one, and I tried to give myself to reading. My eyes pored over printed pages as continually as though reading were a part of their effort to shut out the visible world. The books that I liked, I started over again as soon as I finished them. They were often beyond my comprehension, but my wanting more from them made me capable of giving more of myself to them. I read from the time I came home from school until supper, and from supper until I went to bed. The afternoon hours passed as though none of the events that took place during them existed. When Mother came home from her job and began to cook supper, I was impatient if she called me away from my book. Reading, I saw nothing that went on around me. It was the same as when I slept, and one minute it was night and the next minute morning. But what I read did not disappear the way my dreams did. Also, in retrospect, I seemed to know what had gone on around me while I read, and to know it more clearly than if I had observed it. It was as though someone had written that down and I had read it, too. From not looking, I began to see.

In the evenings when Mother was fixing supper and I was poring over my books, I saw her with a new awareness, as though she were someone I had never seen before, or as though I were a person other than myself. The beauty that I had taken for granted from my childhood was there. But, despite my near-sightedness and the book in front of my nose, I recognized the "double chin" and "middle-age spread" so often referred to in her conversations with my aunts. I saw some enlarged pores on her cheeks where the makeup was not fully removed, and the briefly exposed heaviness of her thighs when she sat on the edge of the bed and removed her stockings. Her clothes, I realized, were the clothes that women choose out of a desire for each other's approval, not those they wear to enhance a beauty necessary to someone who loves them. Her looks were changing, day by day, year by year, and it seemed to me that the life we were living, and not merely the passage of time, was the cause of the change. I felt an urgent sense of loss. Suddenly, I wished with all my heart that she would remarry.

My nearsightedness made me see other things. The first day that I put on glasses, every object became simultaneously clearer and farther away. The distance from my head to my feet increased so much that I walked awkwardly, like someone on stilts. Nevertheless, down on the sidewalk, beside my sharply focused shoes, I discovered cracks that I had not seen before. At school, I caught sight of moles on the necks and chins of my classmates, all the way across the room from me. And in the movies I noticed that the nose of my favorite actress moved up and down like a rabbit's nose when she talked. In time, I probably would have become accustomed to these details and have lost interest in them, but my eyes adjusted themselves to my glasses so rapidly that the details began to disappear while I was still unused to them. As they faded, I made an effort to keep them in focus.

When I raised my eyes from the pages of my book or from my desk at school, where I usually laid my cheek an inch or two from the sheet of paper I was writing or drawing on, it was with an interest in particulars that I had not possessed before. I no longer took appearances for granted.

I began to look more closely at other members of Mother's family, too. Mother did not see her brothers and sisters as constantly as in the past. But the family, except for Uncle Clark, still met frequently, usually for Sunday night supper, and on these visits to the houses and apartments of my various aunts and uncles I saw that none of them felt at ease in any house except his own, just as I had not felt at ease when we used to go to their houses from the homeplace. Then I had seen only that their lives differed from the life that was lived in the house where they had all been brought up. Now I saw that their lives also differed from and resembled each other's, and, presumably, the lives of other people elsewhere. They could be recognized and judged not only by how they deviated from that one no longer existing norm, but objectively, in themselves. They were not just my relatives, they were a small number of the human beings who make up the world.

Like Molière's M. Jourdain, who discovered that all his life, without knowing it, he had been speaking *prose*, I discovered that all my life, without knowing it, I had been living among *people*.

As we went to the houses of these aunts and uncles for Sunday night supper, I also began to see more of my cousins. There were five girls and seven boys among my first cousins, and many more once and twice removed. I did not become intimate with them, but I saw their rooms, their school books, their yards, and met some of their friends. The cousin I liked most was a girl, several years older than I was. Even before we had left the homeplace, she had come face to face with the things I was having my first objective glimpses of, and I had sometimes seen her there crying and talking to my mother about her troubles at home. Her features were delicate and sensitive, and I thought of delicacy and sensitivity as beautiful. But exactly these traits were now plucking out her beauty, the way she plucked out her eyebrows. She wore her hair combed straight back from her peaked forehead, leaving her face bare. Her expression was at the same time a confession and a defiance, and in her eyes I could see reflections of the disapproval and frustration that were enclosing her on all sides. From the conversations of my aunts, I knew that she was "wild," that her mother "couldn't do a thing with her," and that when she was "like that" she "drank." Her features were as delicate as ever, but they had become set, like a mask, from behind which the lost face of happiness looked wildly out of the small openings of her eyes. Her glance moved too quickly in its search for approval or disapproval. Her pleasure in being agreed with was too open. And sometimes I was embarrassed by the intensity of her friendliness.

One Sunday night, as she was telling me how much she liked me and how she used to fight with another of my girl cousins for the privilege of taking care of me when I was a baby, I realized that what I saw in her face was the permanent change from happiness to unhappiness. I had seen the temporary change often—in Mother, in my brother, in myself, in everyone. But I had never before been aware of the profound and visible difference that results when the belief in happiness gives way to the fear that happiness is no longer possible.

To counteract the loss I saw in my cousin's face that night, I searched the features of my aunts and uncles gathered there at Aunt Annie's house for some sign of the gain that would take its place. But what I saw did not make me feel that the loss was justified. I was like a child who is ignorant of war judging returning soldiers. What they had fought for meant nothing to me—only the marks their losses had imposed upon them. My uncles no doubt had striven against conformity, but now they sat motionless in their chairs, as if they had been placed there by someone else. The expression in their eyes was that of husbands who are powerless to speak of what interests them, except when it happens to coincide with the interests of their sisters and wives, or when they escape. Their belts curved comfortably around their heavy waists. They looked trapped—creatures whose basic desires had been anticipated and satisfied before they could pursue them, and who had become aware, too late, that other desires had gradually been substituted for their own.

And what of my mother and aunts, who seemed to control the situation? While their brothers and husbands sat and waited, they moved rapidly about the house, chattering and preparing supper. In their small figures, dressed and aproned for Sunday, and in their practical movements, there was nothing unfamiliar or impersonal. They seemed somehow smaller, as though after the loss of the homeplace they had shrunk to the dimensions of the bungalows and apartments they lived in, and had also, by a concentration of energy, drawn down the size of the world. Their eyes accepted what was around them, taking it in without subjecting it to interpretation, but also without admitting the existence of anything further away.

Aunt Annie was annoyed with Uncle Joe, her second husband, who was an Italian and the only man I had ever seen cooking. He took over the kitchen when they had spaghetti or macaroni. This evening, after looking at the macaroni, he put it back in the oven when the rest of her meal was ready. From the doorway between the kitchen and breakfast room, where I was watching her, I saw her stamp her foot in anger. Then she noticed me, pursed her lips, and smiled. Her smile was in apology for his misbehavior. But when she laughed a moment later, it was at herself, and her laughter seemed to accept, goodhumoredly, how things must be.

"Go up front and tell them to come on back," she said to me. "Joe ought to have enough sense to take up that macaroni in a minute. If he doesn't, we'll just start without him."

As I left, she accompanied me up the hall, taking two short rapid steps to each one of mine, and when we reached the living room, she called out the announcement that she had asked me to make.

At supper, the women helped the men's plates, putting another heaping spoonful on each after they had been told that it was enough.

We ate at the dining room table, with a crocheted cloth and Sunday dishes. Midway of the meal, the conversation touched on Mother's friend, Mr. Dickinson, who had taken us for a drive that afternoon. He had been asked to supper but had been unable to come.

Suddenly, Uncle Tommy turned his pink-and-white face to me and said, "Tell me, Donald, how'd you like to have a new papa?"

I was watching and listening. I longed to hear a discussion of this subject, which I would never have brought up. But wearing glasses, instead of making me feel conspicuous, made me feel that I was invisible, and a question directed to me came as a surprise.

"I wouldn't mind."

No one believed me. I had blushed as though I were lying. And, besides, what I had said was not their idea of what children feel about their parents' marrying again. Mother was sitting next to me. From my lowered eyes I could see two small white scars on her neck just below the hairline, where she had had two moles removed after her hair was bobbed. She did not for a moment think that I was sincere. While she was assuring me that I need not worry, that she had no intention of marrying anyone, my cousin, who was watching me, said:

"I think Donald means what he says. I really think he does."

Mother and my aunts were wearing their good shoes that evening. They slipped them off while they ate, and after supper, when they forced their feet back into the tight, conventional shapes, their expressions were like the expression I had seen earlier in my cousin's eyes. I was not capable of thinking that their view of life was not large enough to contain it, and that by clinging to what was familiar to them in a world that had changed so much since they were young, they were trying to distort and squeeze life into a conception that fit it no better than their shoes fit their feet. Yet they accepted their clothes as they accepted their morality, out of a sense of conformity rather than out of a sense of beauty or fitness. And later, when they took off their shoes in the living room to try each other's on, I was impressed by the shapes of their feet, narrowed into hard and bunioned grotesques.

No doubt I did not reason my family's morality out of their appearances so much as I lent to their appearances what I felt about their lives. Nevertheless, at the same time, an optimistic excitement welled up inside me. I saw more and I felt more. But my feeling of possibility was not the result of my discovering other people and other ways. And my new sensations did not lead to new beliefs, but crowded inside me and made a jumble of the emotions and beliefs already there, the way the last of my permanent teeth, now coming in, crowded and made a jumble of my other teeth, previously straight.

In the absence of people, I sometimes shared my excitement with objects. I used to sit and stare for long periods at the cover of *Story* magazine, so directly and unquestionably plain, with its straight black lines of sans-serif type on dull orange paper, listing the titles and authors of the stories, and nothing else. From my being interested in this magazine and finding in it the names of authors whose books I took out of the library, my reading had begun. I had never read any of the classics most children read;

I hop-skip-jumped straight from the stories to the avant-garde novels mentioned in the advertisements. Since I knew no one who read the books I did, the cover—so different from the illustrated covers of most magazines, and even from the typographical covers of *The Atlantic* and *Harper's*—was, in a way, the friend with whom I shared literature, and I used to sit and stare at it, trying to penetrate its character. Just looking at it strengthened my feeling that the world was more wonderful than the people around me understood, and that they did not ask nearly enough of life.

While this feeling was growing, another important change was taking place beneath it. I was becoming aware that I saw things habitually in a way different from the people around me. By concealing from consciousness what I had seen that night, my psyche had made it unnecessary for me to judge by others' moral standards when I had no standards of my own. Now the disparity between my observations and those of other people slowly forced me to form judgments. I looked at everything with openly curious and accepting eyes, and when my conclusions conflicted with other people's, I did not know how to dismiss my own. It upset me if I found myself at odds with Mother. Nevertheless, it seemed to me that the life around me was being made ugly by circumstances when it did not need to be, and that she and her family, out of an ununderstandable idea of security and morality, were aiding the distorting circumstances. It was as though they all had heard the Devil say "walk a narrow plank straight across the ocean or you will be mine," and all of them, by accepting the challenge, were unwittingly on the Devil's side. They made the attempt, they failed, and they condemned each other's failure. Whereas, I felt that the wrong was to accept the challenge, and condemned the attempt.

This change of attitude took place in me so naturally that I was not aware of what was happening. I knew that I disagreed with the people around me, and that the disagreement was not a matter of generation, for my brother agreed with them, sometimes vehemently. He was even more concerned with security and morality than Mother, whereas security seemed to me to be the limiting of possibility, and a morality based on security to be immoral. In a short time, without outward change, I became a different person and—for practical purposes, according to the standards of the people around me—totally amoral.

I began to feel guilty. I could not see why I was wrong, but I could no more feel right than I could in R.O.T.C. class at school when I was the only one in the platoon out of step. I needed to deny either myself or the people I loved, and I had not the cowardice to do the one or the courage to do the other. My nearsightedness had taught me to look with artificial sharpness at the things around me, but the self-protecting unawareness on which it was based did not allow my sharpsightedness to come close to myself. Neither did it allow me to be aware that I was unaware. The weakness of my vision seemed to affect only what was at a distance. My glasses were made stronger at the end of the first year and again at the end of the second. The lenses remained thin, not nearly strong enough to be distorting, and I wore rimless frames with wire-thin metal temples that Mother told me were not noticeable. Nevertheless, I took them off when

I looked in the mirror. My sense of being at odds with the people around me had created, beneath my other feelings, a dissatisfaction with myself as pervasive as my unawareness, and I could not dismiss my apprehensions.

I did not sleep well at night. The backs of my knees jumped with "growing pains," and it must have been during this time, while I was unaware of them, that my dreams took on the monotonous, semi-frustrated quality of everyday events that was to characterize them later and to keep me interested in the more violent dreams of others. My unknown nightmares probably retained the visual quality they had had earlier. Nearly ten years would pass before I would wake up having dreamed the sentence: "More sins are committed in the name of righteousness than in the garden." A short while after the time I am writing about, however, I began to awake remembering a new recurring dream that throws some light on my protective self-deception. I was in the old family homeplace. Because there were guests, I was sent from my usual bedroom, at the back of the house on the ground floor, to sleep in a room at the end of the upstairs hall. In reality this room had been empty, but in my dream the blond bed from another room on the second floor, used by my cousin Carl, was there. From the far corner of the room, steps went up into the attic where the ghost Bloody Bones lived, and I was afraid to go near the room after dark. It was lit by a dim, newspaper-shielded lamp when I arrived. In the bed an unrecognizable form lay, covered head and all by the bedclothes. Hastening with fear and cold, I undressed and slipped beneath the covers, joining my body to the shape there, in warm and sensual oblivion. Then I awoke.

I could write now, as I came to remember it years later, what I saw that night I walked up the hall and opened the door. But not only was that scene not a part of my life at the time, but a simple description of it would give a misleading impression.

Certain events, like certain words, take on a false emphasis when written down. They convey, from conventions of time and place, meanings they do not have, and fall into categories, as misleading as they are convenient, that permit us to discuss events too upsetting to examine individually.

The moment arrives in autobiography when you ask yourself at what point you must start concealing in order to reveal, at what point you must start lying in order to tell the truth. The answer probably is: at the same point at which you became blind in order to see and ignorant in order to know.

Also, it is possible that what I remember as having seen that night was not merely forgotten during the time it disappeared but was transformed in some way so that, despite its seeming unacceptableness, it became acceptable. I can only trust my instinct of what is true and of what to say. What I saw is best said by what I have written here. After all, my glasses are bought from other people. They are made, like the categories of language, to serve a general need. But my blindness is my own.

The Square Jaw

The year that I was fifteen, I wore braces on my teeth. I did not like the dentist. In my opinion, he was a bad orthodontist. Whether he was or not, it is hard to tell. I eventually pulled off the braces. No one forced me to have them put back on, and the chief difference the year of wearing them made —besides increasing Mother's debts—was two large cavities in the back molars they had been attached to. However, there was one other result. It must have been something the dentist said about correcting my bite that gave me the impression I could change the shape of my face. I decided that I did not have to look the way I looked, and I spent whole days walking around with my lower jaw stuck out.

My appearance, that year when I started to high school, was probably the thing that most recommended me. My features were regular, my skin smooth. More important, my face radiated the glow that youth and innocence shed. But I was unaware of any virtue in my appearance. It was familiar to me, and I had reached the stage where to know something is almost surely to hate it, and to become aware of something new to fall in love with it. Suddenly, all my dissatisfactions with myself and my surroundings centered in my dissatisfaction with my face. In grammar school and junior high school, the other pupils had been from our neighborhood and as familiar as my brother and cousins. At Boys High, the pupils were from all parts of the city. In each class, I was surrounded by students who did not resemble me or any of the people I had ever known. Their unfamiliar and square-jawed faces seemed to preclude the possibility that they were subject to the confusing and dispersing emotions I was subject to, and I wanted to look the way they looked. More than anything else, I wanted to have a square jaw.

The peculiar thing is that I had a square jaw. In this one feature, I resembled the people I wanted to resemble. But I had no idea of it. I would have had to have seen myself from the angle I saw them from for it to have been real to me. And, as I never saw myself that way, I decided that I did not have any appearance at all. Unfamiliarity was essential to my interest. The schoolmates I admired were not my friends. They were not even pupils I would speak to if I saw them away from school. But my reason for not speaking was not that I did not want to. It was my inability to believe that they would recognize me. Since I did not look like them, I decided that I did not look like anything. If I spoke, I feared that they would stare at me without recognition. And I remained silent.

Perhaps, also, speaking to them was not what I wanted. I did not want to know them. I wanted to be them. I wanted, literally, to inhabit their bodies. My regard for my own physical qualities was so small that I did not think that I would lose anything by this. And, since I was as willing to accept that I had no character as that I had no features, I did not think that I would gain anything, either, that was not purely physical. I hardly thought of people as having characters that were not expressed in their bodies, the shapes of their faces, their ways of looking, smiling, moving.

I did not do well in high school. My reaction to studies was as emotional as my reaction to people. In one or two subjects, where I found the teachers sympathetic, my desire to please them was sufficient to make me study hard and be given a passing grade. But the fact that I was good in a subject was no guarantee that I would pass it. One term, I did better than usual in English because I liked the teacher. The next, I almost failed because I was put off by the cold sarcasm of his successor. I memorized other passages of Shakespeare than those he assigned us. I did not even turn in my written work. At home, when my low grades were known, I was exhorted by Mother to live up to the high standards that would be expected of me from the record of my brother, who had never made a grade below ninety. But her exhortations had the opposite of the effect she hoped for.

I received my worst grades in French class. The braces on my teeth made French pronunciation impossible. Whenever I tried the method the teacher suggested, my tongue became entangled in the wires. I was no better in written examinations. During class, my awareness was centered on the square-jawed student who sat opposite me, leaning his head on his desk and thoughtfully sucking the flesh of his forearm. He was the younger brother of a famous high school athlete, who had been graduated the year before and gone on to college, and a perfect full-lipped miniature of him. The French teacher, who was coach of the boxing team, continually remonstrated with him for his not training for athletics, as well as for his not studying. But he was as bored with being told to repeat his brother's athletic record as I was with being told to repeat my brother's scholastic one. His interest was girls. He spent most of his time in class in a dream of events as far away from the athletic field as they were from the wooden portable building we studied in. When he was reprimanded for not training, he answered, with an embarrassed smile, that he preferred going to dances on Friday nights. He blushed and beamed when he was spoken to and had to stand up and answer. Then, when he sat down again, he put his chin and his elbows back on his desk and once more thoughtfully sucked the flesh of his forearm. If he had been more ambitious in his studies, I might have passed French, for I once stole the questions for a coming examination from the teacher's desk and worked out the answers to share with him. As it was, both of us failed.

I almost failed European History, too. My difficulty there was my inability to spell. This, also, was emotional; it had been chronic with me since the day in the fifth grade when I was sent to the blackboard to parse a sentence in front of visiting school authorities. I parsed the sentence correctly, but I was told that I had misspelled a word and must correct it before I sat down. As the classroom clock ticked away, minute after minute, I changed word after word, at first in hope, then in panic. At the end, I lost whatever confidence I had possessed in the correctly spelled words, but I never suspected the misspelled one, *very*, which I had written with two *rs*.

Our high school European History teacher insisted that each pupil pass a spelling test based on proper and geographical names. He was sure that anyone could be taught to spell. Rather sympathetically, he refused to allow anyone to discredit his method. His procedure with me, and with a group of other students that included a dark, square-jawed Polish boy—whose appearance was unlike any other I had seen in that largely Anglo-Saxon part of the world—was to give us the same test of one hundred words over and over. The words never varied. We were told from the beginning that they would not. All we had to do was to memorize them. And there was no possibility of failure. We were made to come back after school and take the test over again until we passed it. I and the dark boy—whose interest was added to for me by my discovery that he owned a white convertible roadster—were among the last pupils there. As the days of the term gave out, we took the test over two and three times an afternoon. Neither my thoughts nor his were on the words. Earnest and eager to be somewhere else, he would glance out of the window of the classroom at his automobile, then clench his pencil tighter in his hand, frown with concentration, and lean over his paper again. And I remember my depression as I sat in the classroom one afternoon, beginning the test once more after even he had passed it. I watched him leave the building and reappear outside, wearing his white sweater with his purple track letter on it, get in his creamy convertible parked on the dark cinder yard between the classroom and the street, cut the gleaming machine in an arc across the cinders and sidewalk to the pavement, twist the wheels straight, and ride off toward Piedmont Park, in the direction of the rich suburb in which I imagined him to live, and toward all the unknown strength and fascination of existing within his body and his life.

I walked to and from school, usually alone. I was not exceptional in this. There were as many solitary figures as there were groups walking away from the large red brick building with its cluster of wooden portables, temporary housing measures of the depression. It is wrong if I give the impression that I was noticeably different from the others. What was outward in my character had not changed since I was a child and everyone commented on how sweet I looked. Most people considered me as incapable of complication as of evil. But an important change was now taking place in me. I was beginning to reason. Many things had given impetus to my self-dissatisfaction. But it was not until I came face to face with the impossible in my desire to look different from the way I looked, and to be a different person from the person I was, that I started to seek logical conclusions from my judgments.

Walking home, out of the crowd of pupils as it thinned into individuals, I figured out that since I did not look the way I liked, and since my desire to change my looks did not change them, I did have an appearance of my own, no matter how reluctant I was to acknowledge it. And, since I admired other people's looks and longed to resemble them, this admiration and longing, if nothing else, gave me a character. But my most important discovery was that I did not dislike having this character the way I disliked having my looks. My approval, considering that I was aware of the short shrift my mother and brother would make of it, was so unlike anything I had been taught to expect of myself that it was, in its way, as interesting to me as the appearances of my schoolmates.

I first became aware of a square jaw the year I worked at the drugstore. The jaw was on a college boy who hung out there and who had broken his arm in an automobile accident that summer. A truck he was driving turned over and the ulna of his right forearm was fractured in four places. His arm was out of the cast when I knew him, and in his right hand he carried a small sponge that he squeezed as an exercise to rebuild his muscles. The sponge was never out of his hand, he never stopped squeezing it, and this solitary activity gave him an abstracted attitude that set him apart from his companions. But he was friendly, and when he saw me he would challenge me to hit him on the biceps of his left arm as hard as I could. This was a kind of game to him, one that he considered beneficial, and when I hit him it put him in a good humor, just as did the tall stories and jokes about sex that constituted the main conversation between his friends and the pharmacists. His friends were especially proud of his having crab lice. Upon their request, he used to lift his trouser leg, awkwardly pick one off his hairy calf with his left hand, and crack it between his fingernails. Then they liked to hear him recite the cure for lice that he insisted was the only effective one for hairy men: You shave half your body; the hairs on the other half, you soak in kerosene; this done, you ignite the soaked hairs, and when the lice come running out of the flames onto the bare flesh, you stab each one with an icepick.

Sometimes when we were playing, he persuaded me to let him hit me in the same way I hit him. He insisted that he would not hurt me, and he never did. But on occasions his blow knocked me off balance and I fell into the newsstand. It was on the newsstand that I discovered *Story* magazine. Until I read it, the idea had never occurred to me that literature was connected to life. But the stories in those pages that I first read there in the drugstore adhered to reality nearly as closely as the square-jawed college boy's lice adhered to his skin. Like his and his friends' tall tales, they were often about "things people don't write about." This lent them the interest of the forbidden. But any blows they gave me hurt me no more than the college boy's did, and they eventually led me to the library and to the books I liked.

This awakening of my literacy did not help me at school. I did worse than ever. When the time came, I was graduated only by adding to my final report card, in an imitation of the instructor's handwriting, a credit for the physical training course that I had sat out in the library, or spent lying on a bank of grass behind the portables watching my square-jawed classmates.

Nor did I get over my dissatisfaction with my appearance. It spread to my body. I was still growing, and as I became taller, I became thinner. The physical training course that I skipped might have helped me to obtain the wide shoulders I came to covet—a feature I did not possess, as I did the square jaw—but while I should have been attending it I was not aware of the desire to change my body. It was during my last year at high school and my first at work that I began to be dissatisfied with my physique as well as my face. And it was not admiring other people's bodies that made me want to share their power. Unlike faces, bodies were covered. It was the desire to do things, to dive, to swim, to lift barrels, that made me want a body ideally suited to doing them. And the examples which made me conscious that the variations in the human body are as great as those in the human face were largely in works of art, in reproductions of paintings and statues, not in people I knew. I did not want to be these works of art, as I had wanted to be my square-jawed schoolmates. Nevertheless, I still wanted something impossible. I was not aware that all men have the same number of muscles, more or less developed, and it was new muscles, the ones that I saw on the people in paintings and statues, and that I thought I did not have, that I wanted. Even physical training class and doing push-ups on the floor at home would not have given me those. But, through the impossibility of my longing, I had stumbled on one of the uses of art. I began to satisfy my desire vicariously.

I had always enjoyed water-coloring picture books. When I had worked at the drugstore, I had bought myself a box of oils and painted portraits of my face as I saw it in the mirror. Now, each of these mediums put too great a technical difficulty between me and my new desire, and I switched to drawing in charcoal and sanguine the autumn I began to take life classes.

The life classes were given by a teacher at Georgia Tech. It was against the college regulations to have nude models on the campus, and twice a week Mr. Ziegler held a life class at his home on Juniper Street near North Avenue. At the Wednesday night classes, for Georgia Tech students, the model was a young woman; at the Saturday morning classes, for artists, a young man. During each session, Mr. Ziegler went around the room, criticizing and correcting his students' work. On mine, on week nights, he diminished the circles of the model's breasts; on Saturdays, he reduced the width of the model's shoulders. I did not think that his changes were improvements. I looked with regret at the shadows of the lines he had wiped out, and at the smaller lines he had drawn in. If I had exaggerated, it was not consciously. But neither was it from a lack of ability to draw what I wanted to draw. And I changed the lines back.

I did not consciously want to draw an ideal. Nevertheless, what I wanted to identify myself with and possess was not perfectly represented by the people who posed. If Mr. Ziegler had chosen his models as I would have chosen them, I told myself, I would have drawn them as he wanted me to draw them. I was in love with precise details, and my love was hopeless enough for me to understand the advantage of being able to represent them accurately. And yet my emotion was not for drawing. It was an emotion so overflowing that it could be expressed by something as simple as running and jumping. I used to express it this way sometimes on the street, filled with a sudden elation. But jumping for joy left me afterward on the sidewalk, the same person as before, longing somehow to stand back and look at my joy. And drawing, to a degree, allowed this.

It was a desire to capture my emotion as well as the object that caused it—a union of the two—that inspired my first attempt to write. It did not occur to me that for the expression of my feelings to be clear my feelings themselves would have to be less confused than they were. It was as the author of a book like the books I had been reading that I saw myself. But neither did it occur to me to imitate the feelings of the authors I admired in order to sound like them. It had to be my feelings that I expressed. There were authors that I would have liked to have been, and I thought about them as I sat down to write, but it was the boy who wanted a square jaw who wrote. He wrote:

THE KELLY BOYS

When I leave this town I shall miss the Kelly boys. I shall miss them more than most of the things here. However the Kelly boys are not friends of mine. In fact I do not know them except from passing them occasionally on Peachtree Street around Tenth Street or watching them as they walk up the aisle in North Side Cafe. I have never spoken to them with the exception of having said hello when I passed them walking with someone who knew them and they spoke. I like to watch them, but from a distance. They cannot be more than vaguely aware that I exist, but they occupy my mind for long periods of time. The Kelly boys are an amazing looking group to be all of the same family. Their appearance I find unimaginable. I am hardly sure that they exist. There are either three or four of them, I am not sure which. There are two blonds and one who is black haired. Perhaps there is another blond, the youngest of the four, who is almost ordinary looking. I am not sure. I have never noticed him if there is. The black haired boy's face is not like the others. You can tell they are all brothers. Their features are all very similar. But the black haired one's face is a little tight and close. He shows ordinary expressions. The others do not. One of the blonds I am told is mildly a sex fiend. At least a girl who goes out with him does not spend a quiet evening. This one is not tall. That is, not tall and lean. He is about six feet but built thick and heavy. His body moves slowly when he walks. With the slow precision of a machine not knowing where it is going and not in a hurry. Maybe he is musclebound. I'm not sure. His face is compact and there are big muscles in it. His skin (all of their skins are like this) is golden, not the color of man's skin usually, with spaces of oranges and reds and tan (the tan that ordinary men get). His hair is the same. Assorted colors. The same gold and brown mixed with the oranges and reds. He has a square face. His face, not his head. And he has lips that form a long rectangle. They look very soft and show no expression. His eyes seem always to be looking a long way ahead, but they do not have a brooding expression. No thought or feeling of ordinary man ever shows on his face. The Kelly boys are all rather dumb and brute, but I am sure that he never thinks as one says a man thinks. Rather he would see the shape of something he wanted and turn it over and feel and examine it as he would hold and feel some part of the body in his hand. And come to know it without being conscious of doing so. But his face instead of being expressionless or blank has an expression that is all expressions at once and mutely says all things. There is his mouth and the hunks of muscles in his cheeks and his nose and his brown eyes under lashes colored like his hair. The thing that makes him a thing of wonder is that you cannot imagine him. You know that he does all the things any man does, but it is impossible to believe that he does these things in the way that everyone else does them. It is as though there is a rock in the sea and you know that this rock does all the simple acts that people do, still you cannot imagine it doing them, sitting on the side of a bed tying its shoe, or eating seated at a table. There is a beauty that you can decide whether you like or not. Everyone does this about certain things, movie actresses or paintings. But with his appearance this is not possible.

One night he was in the North Side Cafe where everyone was drinking beer and talking and the subject of foreign languages came up. He was telling one of the boys how to say something degrading about a person in Spanish and this odd bit of knowledge in his mind was unreal and pointless. It only served to accentuate his removal from such things.

One day I went around a row of lockers in the bath house at Piedmont Park to comb my hair at the mirror and the younger blond was sitting by it dressing. I decided that it would do no good to comb my hair and went back around the row of lockers. I could not stand to be so close to him. And yet I would long to be long in the Kelly boys' company and watch them.

It may sound as though they are a group, always together. On the contrary, they never are. They are always separate. I only see them one at a time. I guess they do not go places together.

Blocks and Books

⊂⊃⊂⊃⊂⊃How do we arrive at what we like and dislike? What interests one person in one thing, and another in another? Why, for example, was I attracted to the authors and books I read and admired in my teens?

As far back as I remember, I liked objects that did not do anything, but that I did something with, pieces of wood, glass, paper. My attachment seems to precede personal associations. Yet it must have begun somewhere.

My taste made it difficult for Mother to be equally generous to me and my brother at Christmas. The year that he wanted an electric train, I wanted a box of water colors. The year that he wanted a bicycle, I wanted a set of colored blocks.

I can still see, feel, smell, taste, and hear those colored blocks. They were inch-and-a-quarter cubes, their surfaces solid squares of the primary colors and black, or divided into two contrasting triangles. They smelled like paint, and if you put your tongue on one there was a faint taste of colored paper. Their lacquer was as smooth as china. They clicked against one another when you shook their box.

The year that I was given them, Mother's brothers and sisters, with their wives or husbands and children, gathered at the home-place for Christmas dinner. The meal was served in relays. When I returned from eating, I found one of my small cousins standing in front of the living room hearth where the open fire had burned down to a bed of coals. One by one, he was throwing the blocks into the grate and watching them as they hissed up into paint-fed spurts of flame, then died down into glowing red lumps, indistinguishable from the coals.

My emotion at the sight cannot be stated in a declaratory sentence. It is enclosed in my sensual apprehension of the event that was happening to those objects, the burning of those blocks. The books that I liked in my teens were books in which emotions merge sensually with the events happening to objects.

My personal concern at the time I began to read—that I saw the world differently from the people around me—was not something that I wanted to explain to others. They were not aware of it. But it was something that I wanted very much to explain to myself.

When you feel this way, you do not need to tell yourself how other people see things. They tell you that all the time. And after a while, you no longer need to question how you see things. You accept that. What you need to explain to yourself is what reality is, which of the two it comes closest to, most resembles. And although this amounts to explaining your viewpoint to yourself, it is an act that changes your viewpoint in the process. Not until you have finished do you know what you are doing.

Long before I learned to name it, I became aware of the difference in tone between a man who is explaining something to himself and a man who is explaining something to others. People who are explaining to others are certain and separate from their subject matter; they can reduce it to declaratory sentences, and there is no confusion in their statements between objects and events. Most of the subjects you are taught in school are taught in this way. But there was an American History teacher in my high school whose tone was different. The first day of the term he told us, "I want to say this at the beginning and get it over with. The War between the States occupies a very small part of American History. We will discuss it when we reach it, not before and not after." Then he spent the rest of the term, day after day, explaining how, despite all appearances to the contrary, the South had won the Civil War. He wanted to be certain that what he was saying was true, but he could never quite put it into words that expressed it satisfactorily. The books I liked in my teens were books in which the author is explaining the subject to himself.

To myself, I needed to explain about girls. I knew that I was expected to marry one and start a family of my own. But I did not share the attitude toward them of the people around me. I could not imagine the girls I liked, and what I liked about them, being discussed by my relatives. And I had never known a marriage that I would have liked to have been my own.

In grammar school, I was "in love" with a full featured, full
figured girl in my class. She tap danced, and when I asked her
for her photograph she gave me a sepia-colored studio portrait
of herself in satin dancing shorts and blouse, a halo of frizzled
hair around her head. That was as far as our intimacy went; I
did not see her away from school. But my attachment was real.
It was strong enough to make me fight off a bigger boy who tried
to take the photograph away from me on my way home. Later,
when I went to a dance in junior high school, I went with a
girl of an opposite type, as shy as I was, and not at all preco-
ciously mature. She would have been highly approved of by my
mother. But, despite her shyness, *she* chose *me*, and I did not
like that. If I had been left to my own choice, and had had the
courage to follow it, I would have gone with the platinum blond
of the school, who one day, when students were asked to enter-
tain the class, stood up before the rows of desks, lowered the
heavily lashed lids of her eyes, and sang in a husky voice:

> And then he holds my hand,
> Mmmmmmmmmm mmmmmmmmmm.
>
> And then I understand,
> Mmmmmmmmmm mmmmmmmmmm.
>
> And then he takes me,
> To par—a—dise.

During high school, the girl who interested me lived on the
next staircase of the housing project where we had moved. She
was half Cuban, and she glowed with a warm coloring of hair

and skin, a sixteen-year-old Latin ripeness of features that made the college boys in the dormitory across the street whistle when she passed. Her eyes flashed straight ahead with anger, and she snapped out rude answers. After a quiet period of sizing up each other, she and I became friends. Her mother worked, too, and during the afternoons I went up to their apartment with her to "study." We lay on the bed in the back room, our books scattered about us on the peach satin spread that matched the shades of the lamps on the vanity table, and kissed.

There was not much to explain about the pleasure given me by her brown eyes, her purplish mouth, and her olive skin with the red highlights upon its extraordinary tan. Nor was there anything to explain about the fact that my mother and brother would consider her as impossible as the other girls I had liked, even as a person for me to be spending the afternoon with. To them she was as unacceptable as the family-approved girls were to me. My thoughts came back to myself. I was the center of the problem. The books that I liked in my teens were books in which the author is also the hero.

This was true of the first book I read on my own, a volume of short stories by William Saroyan. He possessed only this one of the qualities I was to like. But he wrote about a world not unlike the world I knew; he had a familiar tone, that sounded like the tone of someone explaining the world to himself; and he bothered to point out that even when he wrote in the third person he was the leading character. My attachment was total, but brief. In reading, I was like a solitary person first meeting people; he is attracted by the show-offs, but the attraction does not last, for he soon discovers that he takes them more seriously than they take themselves.

The first novel I read was by Aldous Huxley. I discovered him, like Saroyan, in *Story* magazine. He possessed none of the qualities I was to like, but how was I to know it? I read *Eyeless in Gaza*, then *Point Counter Point*. There was no connection between the world I knew and the world he wrote about, and his tone was very much the tone of a school teacher, but I was impressed by his enormous amount of literary name dropping. I felt toward him as I might have felt toward a strange relative from a far place, or a traveling salesman, who suddenly turned up full of unheard-of knowledge: his books were a kind of department store in which I window-shopped.

In each, he had something to say about a man named Proust. In one, he was "that asthmatic seeker of lost time squatting, horribly white and flabby, with breasts almost female but fledged with long black hairs, forever squatting in the tepid bath of his remembered past. And all the stale soap suds of countless previous washings floated around him, all the accumulated dirt of years lay crusty on the sides of the tub or hung in dark suspension in the water. And there he sat, a pale, repellent invalid, taking up spongefuls of his own thick soup and squeezing it over his face, scooping up cupfuls of it and appreciatively rolling the gray and gritty liquor round his mouth, gargling, rinsing his nostrils with it, like a pious Hindu in the Ganges..." The other referred to the "endless masturbation" of the "great book."

Saroyan mentioned the same person; his author-hero "entered the Public Library and for an hour read Proust."

After window-shopping in Huxley, I window-shopped in Davison-Paxon department store. In their book shop, I came upon a four volume edition of the "great book" and persuaded the clerk to let me buy the first volume, on the never-to-be-fulfilled promise that I would return and buy the other three. But before this, I had gone in my turn to the public library, taken out volume one of the eight volume edition of *Remembrance of Things Past*, and read *Swann's Way*. There, for the first time, I encountered writing to which my emotional attraction, in the ways I have mentioned, was complete. The copy I bought contained twice as many pages as the copy I had read from the library, but I started over at the beginning. And when I had read through the whole volume, I started it over a third time. My pleasure had lessened toward the end, but this was not the important thing. The important thing was that in those opening pages Proust presented, as an explanation of the world, the idea that emotions are kept captive in inanimate objects until we free them in an encounter, and he presented this in hypnotically self-addressed sentences that set himself at the heart of his book. *For a long time I used to go to bed early. Sometimes, when I had put out my candle, my eyes would close so quickly that I had not even time to say "I'm going to sleep." And half an hour later the thought that it was time to go to sleep would awaken me; I would try to put away the book which, I imagined, was still in my hands, and to blow out the light; I had been thinking all the time, while I was asleep, of what I had just been reading, but my thoughts had run into a channel of their own, until I myself seemed actually to have become the subject of my book. . . .*

Reluctant to leave my pleasure, I did not want to read the further volumes. No plot, no unfolding of a story, could have interested me the way the merging of those people and objects, those events and landscapes, interested me. There was no more reason to go on than there would have been, in the past, to get a new set of blocks when I still had the old one. Ultimately, I liked books that I wanted to reread, even more than I wanted to reread books that I liked.

Story magazine carried advertisements for James Joyce's *Ulysses*. I tried to take it out of the Carnegie Library, but it was kept in a locked case. Instead, I took out *A Portrait of the Artist as a Young Man*. I could not get through it. I was exhausted by trying to follow the meanings of the words, which seemed too densely put together, as the words in Shakespeare were. (Perhaps this comparison did not occur to me at the time, but it did later when the words in Shakespeare became clear on rereading, as the words in Joyce had.) I returned it to the library and took out *Dubliners*. Here, the words were clear, but the meaning behind them remained elusive. Nevertheless, it was elusive in a way that I recognized, the way myopia made objects elusive, the way my emotions made my thinking elusive, and I felt certain, as I did in life, that what I wanted to understand lay behind the objects presented. I took out *A Portrait of the Artist as a Young Man* a second time. This time I finished it, and the day I returned it to the library I bought a limp-bound Modern Library copy and started it a third time.

The scenes in *A Portrait of the Artist as a Young Man* were often blurred. Sometimes, I did not know where one ended and another began. They left me uncertain of what was going on and who was speaking. But the sensations became my own. The words did in fact what Proust's words stated in theory.

... the white look of the lavatory made him feel cold and then hot. There were two cocks that you turned and water came out: cold and hot. He felt cold and then a little hot: and he could see the names printed on the cocks.

It is hard to isolate sentences. Quotations do not work when they are taken out of context; they are like fish taken out of the sea. I entered the book, and within its context I encountered objects and sensations. Yet I was never hypnotized by the opening sentence, as I had been in Proust. No matter how many times I reread *A Portrait of the Artist as a Young Man*, I did not penetrate the dehydrated infancy of the first half page, recording those years I have no memory of in my own life, and even today the book begins for me with the sentence: *When you wet the bed, first it is warm then it gets cold.*

There was a table of remaindered books in Davison-Paxon, 59¢ and 2/$1. I spent a great deal of time looking through its contents. It was there that I found Gertrude Stein's *Lectures in America*. This was the third book that I made a friend of. Later, I read *Three Lives* and *The Autobiography of Alice B. Toklas*, but I preferred *Lectures in America*. Gertrude Stein was explaining things to herself; she continually made a joke of her attempting to offer her explanation to others, and her foursquare sentences possessed the density and solidity of objects. *One cannot come back too often to the question what is knowledge and to the answer knowledge is what one knows:* this had the tangibility of one of my colored blocks. I felt that I could pick it up, turn it over, and look at its various sides, as she herself did to show: *Knowledge is the thing you know and how can you know more than you do know*; and then: *There is no use in telling more than you know, no not even if you do not know it*; and then: *This is a thing to know and knowledge as anybody can know is a thing to get by getting*; etc.

(Incidentally, I still do not know why I was so fascinated by the colored blocks or why I found them so beautiful; but I do know that seeing them burn did not change my feelings about them. I was as fond of a new set that was bought me the next day as I had been of the old. The blocks by themselves did not recall my emotion at having seen them burn. And I did not hold the burning against my cousin: I have forgotten which cousin it was. My fascination remained; and today, when I am writing, it sometimes seems to me that I am doing the same thing I was doing when I arranged them and that when I get stuck it is not because I do not know the next figure in the pattern but because I am incapable at the moment of finding the block that fills it.)

I was not guided straight to these books I liked. I read, or started, a great many others. In some cases, they were books by authors I would reread and admire when I had developed some measure of literary objectivity. But at the time, the thread that tied me to reading was wholly emotional. My emotions were peculiarly slow in gaining variety, and where they were not concerned I had not the literary tenacity to read even so readable an author as Dickens. (I started and abandoned *The Old Curiosity Shop*, as bored as I had been by all the books I was told to read at school.) I was curious, and out of curiosity

I would search out books, but what I read did not reach very far into my mind except by way of some hidden identification.

One book I bought off the remaindered shelf was Ignazio Silone's *Fontamara*. It bewildered me in a way that other fiction did not. A different curiosity, a glimmering of intellect, stirred in me, but I did not know whom to turn to for elucidation. I was working that summer in the office of the Atlanta Crackers baseball team, at Ponce de Leon Park, answering the telephone and telling callers the score, so the secretary could get on with her work while games were going on. One day, I took *Fontamara* to show to a newspaper man I encountered there. He was a sports editor, but he also wrote editorials and book reviews, and I felt that he would be able to say something that would help me. I showed the book to him when he came in the office and asked if he knew it and what he thought of it. He took it and looked at it. "Yes," he said, "it's all right. But you'd do better to read books by Americans."

He had no idea of my peculiar attitude toward reading, but I wonder what he meant. Would "Americans" in his mind have included Gertrude Stein? Would he have thought that I should not read Huxley, Proust, or Joyce, either? Or even Dickens? The last thing I needed was limitations.

Every Saturday, I walked downtown to the Carnegie Library where, thankfully, fiction was not arranged on the shelves by nationality, and where even the segregation of criticism, poetry, and drama by countries blended together without visible boundaries between 819 and 820, etc. I began to read the whole section of books on literary criticism. For a long time,

I did not question anything I discovered in them. I took the most personal opinions as statements of fact, as though I had become a member of a large family of intellectual people to whom I listened in respect, believing each one while I listened to him, so pleased to be allowed in their company that I did not bother to doubt even when they flatly contradicted one another. I found other writers that I liked, especially poets. Whitman, with his long lists of people and of the parts of the body, was not like the Whitman I had been given an impression of in school. I underlined *And whoever walks a furlong without sympathy walks to his own funeral drest in his shroud.* I repeated E. E. Cummings' *after all white horses are in bed* the way I repeated *For a long time I used to go to bed early.* And gradually, I developed an interest in stories, characters, and plots, and went on to other nineteenth-century books that young people usually read before the twentieth-century ones I had begun with, then came back to those earlier ones with new interest, and went on to others.

I was in the process of transferring the things I cared about to human beings. It was an unconscious process, and carried forward by other means than those I knew of. Earlier, some barrier had limited my feelings for people to my own family, almost to my mother and brother. Perhaps I did not trust anyone beyond them not to abandon me. Now that I was reaching the age to abandon them, an instinct of self-preservation set to work to concern me with other human beings. It achieved this largely through the visual attraction of physical beauty, but it achieved it also, and most importantly, through the development of my emotions into thoughts, my love into understanding. Reading was one of its means, but it had to lead me into books through the paths already at its disposal.

The wonder of beauty is that it does not lie in any identifiable quality. It cannot be isolated; it exists outside the sum of its parts; and until you are aware of it, nothing is wonderful. You do not stand in awe of the moon or stars, of human features or of art. Each thing is simply what it is. The stars are in the sky at night and not in the daytime; one face is different from another; and works of art do not exist as art. They are interesting or not according to whether or not you are interested in their subject matter; they have no aesthetic existence. But once you are aware of beauty, the wonder goes out of it into all that is beyond your understanding. You may make no effort to understand it, or you may track it down as far as "wholeness," "harmony," "radiance." But it remains outside what you can pin down. And from it wonder enters life.

I began to read as the end of something, not as a beginning. Perhaps as an end of objects being satisfying, of beauty being bearable without understanding. There was never any risk of my becoming intellectual. I started too late to be in danger of going too far. It is a happy, ordinary situation. There are no ends now to the books I think good and the books I think bad. But until my literary imagination developed, the only writers I really liked were those in whose books events, objects, and emotions merged as they did in my mind.

A Horse with Wings

◁◁◁A horse with wings. Red. On an oil can outside a filling station on North Avenue. I pass it on my way to work. There used to be one at the Universal Garage on Peachtree Street when I was small. But then it was merely a winged horse. A non-existent thing. Now it is a Pegasus.

I am eighteen and work in the barrel factory attached to the Atlanta branch office of the Coca-Cola Company, behind the main office on North Avenue. My brother is employed in an insurance office and goes to college at night school. Mother has a pleasanter job now at the Coca-Cola Company; she is receptionist at the desk in the main lobby. The three of us live in an apartment at the North Avenue end of the Techwood Housing Project, only a few blocks from the Coca-Cola Company, and as I walk to work each morning there seems little chance that I will ever travel much farther than the corner of North Avenue and Luckie Street, the filling station with the winged red horse, the barrel factory.

My job carries with it the promise that I will be given a position in the office when there is an opening. This is Mother's ambition. I do not want to work in the office. I have never seen anyone there that I would like to be. But I have no alternative to propose, and I live day by day with the knowledge that in the office world I will have no value, and that in no matter what job I am pigeonholed I will have only one thing to give: myself.

I like the factory. The men I work with are unskilled laborers; half are Negroes. Colored and white men work together; a Negro will be on one machine, a white man on the next. But there are separate locker rooms. In the shop, new barrels are made, old barrels are unloaded from boxcars on the railway siding, repaired and relined, and metal drums, which are used, like the barrels, for shipping the Coca-Cola syrup made in the adjoining branch factory, are cleaned and sterilized. Once, for a month in the winter, I painted the raised serial numbers on thousands of metal drums with red enamel.

But I work regularly in the shop where the barrels are made, loading frames of staves in the drying shed and wheeling them to the steam run, riveting metal hoops, boring bungholes in the oak staves of the finished barrels, and when there is a surplus of finished barrels, wheeling them on a flat, six at a time, to the sugar warehouse and stacking them three high. The warehouse is silent and echoing; the shop, with the crashing of heavy iron rings on the cement floor, the screeching of metal on wood as the staves are bent and cut, is so noisy that after the whistle blows at noon and the work stops for lunch, I am deaf in the sudden silence. Beside the steam run, there are fires to char the insides of the barrels, and the summer temperature in the shop is a hundred degrees all day long. I have grown stronger in the year I have been there, and sweated down to hard, lean muscles. But the first summer, when I stacked barrels in the warehouse, I was unable to put up the top row, for this required lifting the forty pound wooden cylinders a full arm's length above my head and then shoving them forward. The Negroes who were in the warehouse, stacking the heavy bags of sugar from the boxcars, or demolishing the stacks and loading the bags on flats to be taken to the syrup plant, did this for me. I like them. I like the white men I work with, too, except for the cigar-smoking foreman. Any contact with office authority seems unpleasant. At the end of the eight-hour day, I go off in one direction and the other workers go off in another. Our lives overlap nowhere outside the factory. What I know of them has a unity of time, place, and action, as classic as that of Greek drama, and a physicalness and simplicity that is Homeric.

It is not from them, however, that I have learned about Pegasus, any more than it is from my family. Nor is it from my literary friends, a third sphere, equally separate from the other two. It is from Butch.

Butch is nearer to the factory workers than he is to my family and friends. Nevertheless, it was among my friends that I met him. But before I tell about that, I should outline, as Greek dramatists do, the events leading up to the main action. How, having reached my late adolescence without any acquaintances not determined by family, neighborhood, and school, did I come to know people I have interests, not place, in common with?

My middle year of high school, a classmate of mine moved into the top floor of the building where we lived on Peachtree Place. I felt friendly to him, for he looked out of his large-lidded eyes onto a world that he understood even less than I did. He lied badly, changing his story each time his mother or grandfather looked dubious (there was no father in his family, either) and one day I saw his older brother hold him while his mother beat him with a hair brush for having walked to his piano lesson, used his car fare to go to a movie, and arrived home late for dinner. He had practiced three hours a day, since he was eight years old, to be a concert pianist, and his family looked upon him as an expensive and incomprehensible investment. In the afternoons when they were all away, he would occasionally throw his head back, his shoulders forward and, smiling at the ceiling, delight himself by playing us one of the pieces of popular music that he was forbidden. Then he would return to his practicing until, in a burst of high spirits, he rushed back to the kitchen, teased the Negro maid, and finagled her into giving us a taste of something that she was preparing for supper.

One night, when he and I had been to a movie and were drinking a beer afterward at the North Side Café, a friend of his from the piano company where he took his lessons introduced us to a poet whose work I had read and liked. The poet was employed as an actor by the local unit of the Federal

Theatre Project that had opened in Atlanta that year. He lived a bohemian existence, and even the friend who introduced us looked slightly askance upon him. But he was the first person I had known that I could talk to about reading. After that, if I saw him sitting on the terrace of his garage apartment on Fifth Street when I was on my way home from school in the afternoons, I would stop and speak to him. Soon, I was going to parties there on weekends. Most people connected with the theatre and writing, and with the vagrant fringes of life around them, turned up at the apartment sooner or later. One night, after I had started working at the barrel factory, Butch came with a man who had been a candy butcher at the Atlanta Theatre in the days when it was a burlesque house.

The boy who shared the apartment with the poet had snapped the button off the bathroom light switch in the entrance hall between the two rooms that evening, and when Butch arrived the poet commandeered him to fix the broken switch.

From the front room, I could see him working in the hall. He was short, heavy-built, black-haired, and younger than any of the other guests, except me. He wore a hound's-tooth sport jacket, sharp in style, and a brown turtle neck shirt. As he leaned against the wall with a screw driver in his hand, smiling at the poet, there was something disconcertingly out of place about him.

While he was working, a Negro man arrived at the front door with a block of ice. I took the ice and put it in the tub in the dark bathroom. As I did, Butch finished refastening the switch and flicked it up and down several times, casting the bathroom from darkness to light and back again.

I did not think that Butch was someone I could be friends with. Despite my working in the factory and our living in the housing project, I was the most middle-class of the people who came to the garage apartment. I belonged to the weekend part of that world. When we were introduced, he called me "Four-eyes," and someone who found it that unusual to meet a person wearing glasses was not likely to be interested in me.

I sat down on the floor by the woman who was the business manager of the theatre. The poet was taking up a collection to buy a bottle. Butch was standing nearby. I tried to think what was out of place about him. He was neither handsome nor ugly. His brown eyes were of the kind that remind you of an animal, in no matter how intelligent a face they appear, and he had a way of standing, as though offering himself to be admired, which gave him a quality of being himself, and nothing else, that added to my feeling that I could not talk to him. Then the poet finished taking up the collection and asked Butch to go for the whiskey. Butch turned and asked me to go with him.

We drove in his automobile to the edge of the business section and parked across the street from an old frame residence with a neon sign outside saying HOTEL. Other guests rode with us, but only Butch and I entered the building. When we were in the entrance hall, he assumed the grave air of a hierophant introducing a candidate into a sacred mystery. There was a desk, as in a hotel, but there were no rooms for rent. The

man from behind the desk took us down the hall to an un-
furnished room where another man produced two quarts of
whiskey from a closet. Butch examined the unfamiliar labels
and said that they were all right. Then the man put the bottles
in a brown paper sack and Butch led the way back outside,
waiting until he reached the sidewalk to smile.

When we arrived at the garage apartment, he ran in, taking
long strides with his knees bent, like the comedian, Ben Blue,
and handed the bottles to the poet.

It does not suffice to say that I liked Butch. From that night,
he was for me an object that is also an event. I looked upon
him, also, as though he were a rock in the sea that unimaginably
does all the things a man does. But my inability to imagine him
doing them was dispelled by my doing them with him. My
attachment was complete. As in my mother I loved everything
that had always been, that was close, and known, and secure,
in Butch I loved everything that was new, that was coming into
being, and the excitement that was yet to be.

I do not know why a person so open was so extraordinary
to me, or how, despite our differences, he accepted me. He
was two years older than I was, the same age as my brother,
and like me he had grown up admiring his older brother. But
his affection had not died, as mine had. When he was seventeen, his brother committed suicide, and he shut out his grief
in some way that added to his awareness. As a result, his attitude was tough and at the same time touched by perception
and understanding. He had run away from home a number

of times when he was younger; but since his brother's death, except for a single trip to New York, from which he had just returned, he had stayed in Atlanta. He ran a sign shop, and for a while he had done the marquee work for the Federal Theatre. His background was as woman-filled as mine. His father was dead. His mother and two sisters lived in Atlanta. He did not live with them; they had been poor when he was small, and he had been adopted by an elderly lady and her maiden daughter when he started to school. Nevertheless, he saw his family all the time he was growing up. Every weekend, his brother telephoned and said that he was the scoutmaster and that he was planning an overnight camping trip. Then Butch met him and spent the night where they went to a party, or where his mother was living at the moment. She moved every time the rent was due in those days. When the landlord was not looking, as Butch put it, she piled as many of her possessions as she could on her sewing machine, the only thing she owned with wheels, and wheeled them over to a new place.

Until he and I met, the only people I had known at the poet's were people I resembled and had some goal in common with. Butch was the goal. Yet he liked me. I think of Mohammed and the mountain. If the mountain would not come to Mohammed, Mohammed would go to the mountain. We were both Mohammeds, both mountains, and both willing to move.

While he was fixing the light switch, I had noticed his coloring. Later, as I listened to him talk, the shape of his head and features, his smile and his eyes, sometimes almonds, sometimes half moons, seemed to become a part of his words. He did not look as though he had lived the life he described. His body was as compact and muscular as a factory worker's, but from what he said it was obvious that he did not owe his build, as the factory workers did, to exercise. And I saw what was disconcerting about him. He was tough, but at the same time he was innocent. His innocence owed nothing to inexperience, but his dissipation had left no more mark on his body than if it were the body of a statue endowed miraculously with life. No doubt, he did all the things he said, and was as tough as he appeared, but at the same time he beamed with the smile of a twelve year old.

He asked me if I had ever run away from home.

"Once," I said. "I came back when it got dark."

"Most kids do," he replied. "I wanted to come back the first time I ran away. But I'd left on my bicycle, and I was fifteen miles out in the country. So I stopped at a farm house and asked them to put me up for the night.

"I can remember the breakfast they gave me in the morning," he added. "The biscuits that were so big around, and the sausages, and the syrup, and the flies. I didn't know there could be so many flies. And nobody else paid any attention to them. Then, when breakfast was over, the woman put all the food that was left in the center of the table and folded the cloth over it. That was so if any of the men got hungry in the middle of the morning, he could have a snack. And the cloth was to keep off the flies."

He paused with his air of waiting to be admired.

"After breakfast, I wanted to go back home. But I didn't feel like bicycling another fifteen miles, so I tried a ruse. I pushed my bicycle into the red clay gully at the side of the road and lay down on top of it. Pretty soon, a car full of men stopped and picked me up. I don't remember what I told them. That I'd been hit, or was sick, or something. They were a bunch of hunters. They all needed shaves. And they drank all the way back to town."

With Butch, impulses led immediately to action. I thought, in those days, that he was wholly objective. In retrospect, I think he was so subjective that it came out in reverse as objectivity. No hint of impersonal judgment interfered to confuse his clear view of the world as he saw it. He watched and listened, and his mind embraced and made use of everything. Only when he tried to "think"—a process he admired in me, but which he considered artificial, and which was artificial for him, for he was so inside his mind that when he tried consciously to go inside it he went outside into some arbitrary sequence of ideas—did he become confused. But he seldom did this. Most of the time he was happy to "plan," a process he carried out effortlessly and intelligently.

We began to see each other every weekend. Every weekend was an adventure. The worlds he introduced me to overlapped with others. My uncles might have turned up at the bootlegger's house in the country, its yard full of English bulldogs, that we visited one night. My cousins might have picked up the waitresses we picked up at the watermelon stands on

Ponce de Leon Avenue. But neither of these would have come to the poet's apartment. And the poet and his friends no longer follow where we go, roving around town in the old black 1933 Ford sedan. Our relationship is as particular as Butch's character.

Saturday mornings, when the barrel factory is closed, I walk downtown to the Carnegie Library, then meet him for lunch. He does not have his sign shop any longer and he works in the display department of a large store, lettering show cards. But his situation at work is the opposite of mine. He is a craftsman. In his job, he can give his skill and keep his life for himself.

Late on Saturday afternoons, we drive to Macon where we have a group of friends we met in the spring. The mixture of people in Macon is exciting. Most of them are richer than we are. The young men own collections of books and prints. The girls are prettier and more refined than those we know in Atlanta. On Saturday night, we go to a roadhouse and dance. The pleasure is rich and warm, like the colored lights of the juke box. But on Sunday mornings, when, having been drunk, and made love, and slept, I wake up as though being born again, pure, whole, and with the physical world of flesh and flowers before my eyes for the first time, and we sit around and do nothing in particular but talk, the different parts of my life come near to each other, and my joy in being alive is so great that I can no longer comprehend that my life will be as narrow as the future I know is in store for me.

Macon is in the direction of the coast, southeast. On the way there, as we drive through the long deserted stretches of the trip, I think of the ocean where I was photographed on the shore when I was six months old and we lived with my father, but which I have not seen since. I would like to see it. But Macon is less than half way, and we never go farther.

On the trip, Butch sings me a song he learned from his brother.

> Oh son, oh son,
> Where did you get
> The blood on your shirt sleeve?
>
> It is the blood
> Of the little pony
> That plowed the furrows for me.

Or one that his mother used to sing.

> Go tell Aunt Tally,
> Go tell Aunt Tally,
> Go tell Aunt Tally,
> The old gray goose is dead.
>
> One she'd been saving,
> One she'd been saving,
> One she'd been saving,
> To make a feather bed.

Sometimes he tells me one of his dreams.

"I was going somewhere with my brother. He was dead, and I knew that he was dead. But the two of us weren't thinking

about that. We were going to the hospital with a woman who
was about to have a baby. We were over in the old part of town
where the tree roots break up the sidewalk, when the woman
suddenly lay down on the sidewalk and had twins. They were
dead, but it didn't bother her. She just rolled them down a
bank and walked off. Then we were in a field. It looked like
the country, but it was the city because the brick building of
O'Keefe Junior High School was on the horizon. The place
was a dump heap, the kind of dump heap children like to
play in, you know, and there were a whole group of children
running over the piles of garbage, rolling hoops. Some of the
hoops were ordinary size, but some of them were larger than
the children, eight or ten feet high. Their tops circled up into
the sky, and you could see the mist and moving gray clouds
through the arcs. Some of the hoops were eaten with rust and
had breaks in them, but they rolled over the breaks as though
they weren't there. There was a lot of smoke, hanging low
because of the dampness, although I don't remember any fire.
Then six or seven men, all wearing turbans on their heads, like
Hindus, came out of the smoke toward us, and I woke up."

It was on one of these trips that we stopped for gas and saw
a winged red horse on an oil can in the filling station and he
recited:

> The Pegasee,
> The horse that had wings for to flee.

He did not remember when he had heard it. But later, in
Macon, where no one knew the rhyme, but where they laughed

and said that the word was Pegasus, he insisted that it was "Pegasee," for it had rhymed with "flee."

Mother is not pleased with what she knows of the way I spend my time with Butch. She thinks that I should go to college at the University of Georgia's Extension Night School in downtown Atlanta, as my brother does, studying for a degree in Commercial Science. A college degree is important. Even people already in the Coca-Cola Company office, who do not have one, go to night school and study to get ahead. She cannot understand my lack of ambition. And I cannot reply that I have an inverse ambition. I cannot say that although I do not like getting ahead, I like looking at people. That although I do not like studying, I like the odor of people. That although I do not like the Coca-Cola Company, I like the touch of people. I do not yet know that it is discovering things for myself that interests me. But I do know that the goal she holds up to me attracts me even less than the means of attaining it.

When we do not discuss my future—when I am still for her the little boy, afraid of the dark, who called out at night, "Mo-ther!" and when she came and asked what I wanted, answered, "I lo-ve you,"—we enjoy being together.

It is not dark for several hours after she and I come home from work. The windows of the apartment look out over North Avenue to the football stadium of Georgia Tech and the evening sky. While she cooks supper, I sit in the window and talk to her through the open door of the bedroom, where there are twin beds for my brother and me and where Mother, who sleeps on a studio couch in the living room, has her dressing table. Then she and I eat, and she puts a plate in the oven for my brother, who is attending night school classes at the summer session, too, so he can finish four years work in three.

"Lean toward me," Mother says. "Why, Donald, there's a white hair in your head. And you won't even be nineteen until next week!"

"I know," I say. "I've seen one before."

"You inherit that from your daddy," she says. "He had gray hairs the first time I saw him."

This is the only resemblance to my father she ever points out in me; the others she remarks are in my brother.

She and I have come to share the same sense of humor. Sometimes, we start laughing over nothing and cannot stop. It does not happen as often as it did a year or two ago, when this was our first way of sharing experiences as two adults, not as mother and child. But there are still evenings when we sit on the upholstered chair and hassock in the living room, holding our sides with the pain of too much laughter, each begging the other not to make him laugh any more, and each helplessly, almost silently, going on laughing.

Or we take walks, arm in arm. Mother has a blue eyelet dress this summer. At no other time is it so blue as it is when we pass the pink crepe myrtle bush near the entrance of the apartment at twilight. But ordinarily, there is no place for us to go. We walk to the corner and turn up North Avenue, past the motion picture theatre and the run-down college boarding houses. We return and mount the stairs of the entrance hall, with its tile walls, cement stairs, and metal banisters. Mother washes out some clothes. I read. When my brother comes home, he studies in the bedroom with the light on until after midnight.

Every summer, the Coca-Cola Company Club gives a party. This year, it is at the Brookhaven Country Club. I go with Mother as her "date." Everyone is there, from the President of the Company and the Board of Directors down. Here is the world I will enter, gathered at a hundred tables on the terrace, overlooking the twilight of a golf course that slopes down to a lake. There is not as much variety as there might seem. Everyone plays the conventional representation of himself. I sit with Mother and a group of her friends. I dance with her. All evening, people seek her out to tell her a joke, to introduce their husbands or wives. I realize how much she likes these people, how naturally her conviviality has flowered among them, and what a delight she is for them to be with. She is a little restrained by my presence. But only a little, like a young girl with her brother along on a date. Mothers with sons are as natural here as husbands with wives. I could fit into this world very well —at the price of playing its representation of myself. But I know that I would tangle with its chimeras. And the sight of that combat would wound my mother beyond recovery.

From my birthday on, Saturday by Saturday, the seemingly haphazard events of the summer move toward a single end.

The poet has left Atlanta for a job up North. There is no longer the garage apartment to visit. But some of our friends from the closed Federal Theatre, including the woman who was business manager, have rented apartments on Baltimore Block. This row of buildings is unique in Atlanta. The three-story houses are joined and flush to the sidewalk, with stoops leading up to the entrances half a story above the street, and a single carved cornice extending across the long façade. Butch says they are like buildings in New York. But they are unlike anything I have seen except brick stores on the squares of small country towns. When they were built, before the turn of the century, the residential section of Atlanta had just started moving away from the state capitol, out toward the north side of town. They were fashionable, their difference was an attraction, and they were pointed out to visitors as one of the sights of the city. But the business section, trailing northward, has long since overtaken them. The buildings have not been single-family residences for many years, and during the depression most of them were empty, vagrants sleeping in their doorways. Now, a decorator and a photographer have moved into the block. It is becoming a collection of brothers to the garage apartment. The rent is cheap. Single rooms are available, and no lease is required. If you want a place, you take it by the month and do whatever repairing and decorating you like. One Saturday night when we are visiting there, Butch has a plan: we will rent a studio of our own. We look at a room on the top floor of one of the middle buildings, and the next Monday he goes to the agent and pays the fifteen dollars for the first month. Mother is dubious about my being involved in this studio. She is suspicious enough of my reading when I do it at home, and she does not see why home is not the best place for me to work at my drawing. But she agrees, not knowing how to object successfully.

During the week at work, I am called to see the plant manager. It is not, as I fear, to be told that I now have an office job, but to be informed that since I have been working more than twelve months I am entitled to a one week vacation. However, since I am the last on the list to be appointed a time, it will not be until fall. On Saturday, while Butch and I are cleaning the studio to paint it, we talk about vacations. The theory behind them seems to me immoral. It makes pleasure into something separate and artificial, the way convention has made beauty into something ornamental and ugly. You work a year, then, just when enough pressure has been accumulated to bring about a change, you are given a one week vacation to let off steam. Mother went to New York on a guided tour for her vacation in the spring. My brother is going there in the week between the summer and fall terms at night school, to see the World's Fair before it closes. I plan to spend my vacation here in the studio, doing the ordinary things I like.

Butch's mother has bought a refrigerator, and the next Saturday, in exchange for our painting her kitchen for her, she gives us her old ice box. We put the ice box in the automobile and take it to Baltimore Block to add to our other piece of furniture, a mattress the two ladies Butch lives with have given him. Betty, his sister, comes along and watches us carry the ice box up the steps to our studio on the top floor. Then we go downstairs into the parlor floor apartment where an old woman has died during the week. Her relatives have closed up the apartment until they can go through her possessions, but Butch knows how to open the lock. We tiptoe inside. Nothing has been touched. We feel like housebreakers, and, awed by the recent presence of death, we go through the dark, shade-drawn rooms, looking at the bottles of medicine on the bedside tables, opening drawers full of old cosmetics, picking letters out of the fireplace grates full of torn-up bills and used envelopes. Betty holds on to Butch's shirt tail, saying she is afraid. Suddenly, there is a noise from the street. We rush out and upstairs to our room. Laughing, happy to be alive, we sit on the mattress beside the ice box and have a drink.

A summer downpour. We have been painting the studio, but we stop. The roof leaks. Water is coming through the ceiling. We move the mattress and put an empty paint bucket beneath one of the dripping spots. While I wait, lying on the mattress and reading, Butch goes to see the agent. When he returns, he says that the agent will do nothing. The roof is our responsibility. And the roof is in such a bad condition that it will take a lot of money to find and repair all the leaks.

We go out and eat supper with our friends and talk a long time about what should be done. When it is late, we return to the studio with a bottle. The rain has stopped. By the glow of the bare light bulb, we look at the stains and leaks. Butch has drunk too much. In disgust, he goes to sleep on the mattress. I cannot wake him. Or, at least, he will not answer when I shake him, although I believe that he is awake and wants oblivion. I say that if he does not answer I will leave. This has no effect, and I go. At home, I undress and get in bed. But I cannot sleep. What if I should not have left Butch lying unconscious on the floor? In the dark, I dress and leave the apartment and walk to Baltimore Block. Butch's automobile is in front of the building, but the door is locked and I have no key. I ring the bell. He does not answer. I call him, but I cannot get into the building. After nearly an hour, I sit in the automobile and wait. He finds me there when he comes down early in the morning.

Saturday, the 16th of September. When I am ready to go out in the afternoon, I find a letter from the Housing Project office slipped under the door. The letter explains that the income of a family in the Techwood Homes cannot exceed a certain multiple of its rent, and that the combined incomes of Mother, my brother, and me, now exceeds it. We must move by the first of October. Mother is playing bridge at the Elk's Club, but I know that something must be done immediately and I telephone her. She comes home weeping. As soon as one problem is solved, she laments, another begins.

We do not have much trouble finding a place to move. A man at the Coca-Cola Company tells Mother that there is a vacancy in the building where he has an apartment. It is on Peachtree Street, farther north than the homeplace was, beyond Pershing Point. The tall cream brick apartment house sits back from the street on a hill of green lawn; it is a light, well-kept building, and the vacant apartment is at the back of the L-shaped structure, looking out onto a lawn and over a hedge into the garden of an old residence next door, rundown and overgrown with oak trees, as our yard was when I was a child. The rent is not too much more than we have been paying, and Mother will have a ride to work in the mornings.

Butch and I have not paid the second month's rent on Baltimore Block and do not have the studio any more. There is still Macon to go to, but these changes make the different parts of life in Atlanta seem more and more separate. I know passion, interest, and pleasure separately. I long to know them together. I want life to be a single thing, not divided into work, home, and friends, all at odds. I have made a linoleum block cut of the head of Michelangelo's David; Butch has printed it for me on his press at work. I shower with the body each afternoon at the factory. In Macon, one weekend I dance so often with the same girl that suddenly there is a scuffle between Butch and her boyfriend, who wants to hit me over the head with a bottle. My glasses are off and I know nothing about it; but I have discovered about the beautiful what, later, I will discover about the young: that there are always more of them. The progression from thinking that what I love is beautiful, to loving what I think beautiful, has given me a certainty that a dozen years of Sunday school and church never gave me a hint of—that life is spiritual. The realization that after I am gone other people will feel the emotions I have felt about the objects I have seen, fills me with an awareness of immortality greater than the idea of life after death. No doubt, what is ugly persists as well as what is beautiful, and hate as well as love, but it is the understanding that qualities persist in individuals, while individuals expire, that draws me out of myself.

We move into the new apartment on the last day of September, a Saturday. Aunt Ada helps us in her automobile. Mother is glad to be back near the neighborhood she lived in when she was young. But we are in a different world. The only objects we still have from the homeplace are the twin beds and a few photographs and pieces of china. As we try to find space in the closets for everything that has to be put away, and to arrange the studio couch and the overstuffed chairs in the living room, the reactions of the people in the office are equally important with the reactions of Mother's brothers and sisters, which would have been the only considerations in the past. The conversation that accompanies our activity is more about the office than it is about the family. There is a rumor that this year the company will give a Christmas bonus of a whole month's salary. It will be given to the factory workers, too, but Mother says how much nicer it will be if I am in the office by then.

Butch and I talk sometimes about my prospects. To him, the solution is simple. What you do not want to do, you do not do; and what you do not like, you change. He is selfish; but selfishness, when it is basic and healthy, does not bother new relationships, and it causes no trouble between the two of us. Anyway, I would rather talk about him. More and more, I like to hear his stories about his brother. The Greeks, I will read later, believed that early in life some tragedy must be undergone, gathered in a handful, and understood, and that, finally, death itself must be experienced in some memorable form. On my own, I realize how important it is that no one close to me has died. My father is gone, but he is alive some-where. Death is not in the graveyard, but here. Life is not where I am, but in some far place, outside conventions, proprieties, securities. I know that I lack some important and final ex-perience which gives the ability to say *no* to certain aspects of life, without which the ability to say *yes* to others does not exist. Butch has had this experience in as memorable a way as possible. I realize that this is one thing that makes him different from me, one thing that gives him the power of action that I lack, and I lend myself to his emotions about his brother with the intensity of an organism vicariously experiencing a necessary mutation. Also, despite my acceptance of myself, I have not lost my desire to be other people, too.

Butch has begun to "think" about his job in the department store. In his work room, off the display department, he runs the line-o-scribe machine, letters show cards, and does airbrush work. He is at the call of half a dozen people in different de-partments. His idea is to be difficult to them before they have a chance to be difficult to him, and he has taken to telling them to go away and leave him alone when he is busy on a job for someone else. He can get along with most of them, he says, but he does not like the manager of the store, who runs from department to department, putting in his two cents everywhere.

In mid-October, I am called to the office again. Once more, it is not what I fear, but to be given the date set for my vaca-tion, the next-to-last week in November. I plan to telephone Butch in the evening and tell him, but he telephones while we are eating dinner. He has been fired. Half an hour later, he comes by for me in his automobile. Riding around, we discuss what has happened. That afternoon, the manager came into his work room and told him that he had to be more cooperative, immediately, or he was fired. He laid down the show card he was lettering, lit a cigarette, put on his coat, and walked out. At home he has an airbrush from the store that he was repairing and he is going to keep it.

We go by the business manager's apartment. Some of her friends are with her and they talk about New York. Despite Butch's having been there, he does not know anyone in New York. The people he stayed with, the summer before we met, have returned to Atlanta. But he is full of the subject, and he talks to me about it after we leave Baltimore Block and are riding home.

The next Saturday we tell our families that we are going to Macon. We rent a room in a hotel downtown. Butch has a plan: we will go to New York. We can go on my vacation. My mother will agree to the trip, for both she and my brother have been there. Then I will write and say that I have a job and will not come back. He will do the same thing. We will need money to live, for good jobs are even harder to get there than in Atlanta, and we spend a long time making a list of the ways we can gather funds.

Monday, Butch starts working again, this time at McCrory's 5¢, 10¢ and $1 store. The Thanksgiving and Christmas rush has begun. The display department is keeping long hours, and he stays and makes overtime every night. The store has never had so willing an employee before. His behavior is the opposite of what it was at the other job. The manager is so pleased that he says he will give him a permanent position after the holidays if he wants it. Also, Butch tells me that the other store has had to hire two new men to replace him.

Saturday, we meet downtown for lunch and talk over our progress. I have paid Mother my rent for the month and have put the rest of my paycheck into my savings account, which I will draw out when we leave. And I have brought my typewriter downtown to lend to Butch, so we can take it with us to New York without arousing Mother's suspicion. He has put an ad in the newspaper to sell the automobile. He owns it with a friend, but he will take the down payment. We talk all through the meal, yet somehow our plans seem intangible, and after we have eaten, in order to commit ourselves with something actual, we go across the street from the cafeteria and enter a cheap luggage shop. It is a narrow store. Suitcases and trunks are stacked from floor to ceiling. We ask to see the cheapest suitcases. The proprietor puts several on the counter for us to choose from. We decide on a tan one, finished in imitation cloth, and say that we will buy two alike. They cost seven dollars each. We pay two dollars down and promise to return with another payment the next week.

Mother has agreed to my going to New York on my vacation. It is odd of me to go after the World's Fair has closed, but it is just one more of the meaningless things I do, like renting the studio for one month. My lack of aim in life is becoming so usual in her eyes that there is no point in harping on it each time. Nevertheless, she is concerned that I do not have an overcoat. Butch, who has two, lends me one. I take it home so she can see it and not be worried that I will be cold. As for our missing the World's Fair, the prospect of missing a public event like that gives us a private joy. We think with pleasure that we will not be in Atlanta for the much-heralded December opening of the movie of *Gone With the Wind*, with "debutante balls," "cinema stars," and "Atlanta society in full dress."

The weather is changing. The fruit on the persimmon tree in the yard next door, which has somehow survived the change of this terrain from woods to city, sets the color of the changing leaves. During the week it grows cold, and the automobile is sold. The night that Butch is to deliver it, he has a flat tire. There is no jack in the automobile, and he does not call a garage. He drives on the tire to a filling station where they change the tires and put the cut-up one in the spare case. He was on his way to a pawn shop to pawn his grandfather's watch when he had the flat, but the pawnbroker offered him so little for it that he has decided to take it to New York with the airbrush and hock them there.

Saturday. Armistice Day. In anticipation, we buy our one-way bus tickets and make our reservations. The fare is $17 each; the trip takes thirty-six hours. We will leave at nine o'clock on next Saturday morning, the 18th, and arrive in New York after dark on the night of the 19th.

During the last week, my separation from the people around me develops as never before. I am incredulous that they believe in this one-week excursion, a thousand miles and back, by bus. They are supposed to be the sensible ones, not me. Money means freedom or security, but how can they believe that I will spend this much of either on a round-trip ticket that will bring me right back where I started? Yet they believe, as they will believe later that I have found a job. I act as I must, and I am believed in because of the innocence of my face. But the horse of the muses is a physical thing, all flesh and blood, not ethereal ideals.

Both Butch and I work on the Friday before we depart. That night, I pack my new suitcase. It is the first that I have owned. You do not need a suitcase when you are going away from a place, I tell myself, only when you are going toward one. I go to bed for the last time in the twin bed. I even go to sleep. In the morning, I eat one of the big breakfasts that Mother cooks on Saturdays and Sundays. She telephones for a cab to take me to the station. We watch for it from the stoop of the building. I am wearing Butch's overcoat. The cab appears from the back of the driveway, which goes in a circle around the apartment house, and draws up to the steps leading down from the lawn.

I kiss Mother goodbye and leave. At the bus station, a friend has come to see us off. He is sure that we will be back by Christmas. I am sure that we will not. We check our bags and see them put safely in the bus. At a liquor store across the street, we buy four flat pints of Carioca rum, put one in each pocket of our overcoats, and pin the pockets with safety pins. Butch's sister and another friend are in the station when we return. Then the bus driver is warming the motor.

The bus rolls down Carnegie Way and out of town. In the bright sunshine, each familiar building, conscious of being seen for the last time, rivets itself to the street. Frame houses, factories, signboards approach, stamp themselves, and are gone. We pass Buckhead, five miles out, where I used to ride each day on the streetcar when I was a curb boy at Hawk's Drugstore. We pass Athens, seventy miles farther, a rest stop. Just over the state line in Anderson, South Carolina, where I once went for a summer visit as a child, we stop for lunch. Then we enter a new world.

I have not thought of the long monotonous eastward stretch of the Carolinas as forming a part of the trip North, but they loom up and go on and on, the way unforeseen sensations loom up in my feelings. In this bare new country, everything is reversed. Butch and I are leaving, but we seem stationary, with the landscape fleeing behind us. I am losing all I know, but I feel only gain. I am forming cataracts of unhappiness over my mother's eyes, but I think of the unhappiness I am saving her by not remaining. And somehow, I remember my grandfather and great-grandfather and the world they went forth to encounter after the Civil War, and I feel nearer to them than to the intervening generation, all of whom will live out their lives in the city where they were born, near enough to visit one another each day.

Toward evening, the bus draws into a supper stop. From the platform, we walk up a ramp into the café, a room painted dark blue, with panels of silver wallpaper. We sit at the counter and have sandwiches and coffee, then we go out of the swinging doors of the street entrance. A five-and-ten-cents store is on the opposite corner. We cross and buy a jigger, so we will not have to drink out of the bottles. Daylight is paling and blueing. A few lamps are lit along the street. When the bus curves out of the station, past a block of liquor and hardware stores, the trees are black and bare against the pale sky. Hesperus brings the night. In the headlights, the trees are pale against the black country sky. It is dark inside the bus. The whine of the tires on the concrete weaves a white line along the highway. We have a drink from the jigger, let back the seat, and close our eyes.

Somewhere, in the middle of the night, we are awakened. It is cold. The station is an old red brick building with a Civil War air. Half asleep, we stand by the pot-bellied stove and warm ourselves, holding the typewriter and watching to see that the suitcases are transferred. In the new bus, we cover up with the overcoats and try to go back to sleep. But already, in the vagrant closeness of the moving bus, I feel the anonymity of New York, the opposition that is true friendship, that does not oppose as I believe that Atlanta does, by offering revolt as the one-way street to conformity, but by placing you in the middle of the extreme possibilities of yourself and making you choose which you will move toward.

I can smell the rum on Butch's neck. My hand touches his arm. Clusters of neon, fading in the country night, like socks running in a basin of water, forecast Manhattan's sky. There, overcoats will not be enough to warm us, only a whiskey and free lunch at a White Rose Bar, or a Nedick's breakfast, with two doughnuts, in the cold joy of a street where thousands and thousands of people pass, not one of whom cares if we eat or starve, live or die. After approaching all day across tomorrow's traffic circles, suburban business sections, and elevated highways, we will walk out of the 51st Street bus station into the night of Eighth Avenue, where people live above stores and bars, but you cannot see how they get to their rooms. When we ask directions, the answers will be in meaningless terms of uptown and downtown, east and west. Nothing will be separate, nothing will conform. Tenements will be a block from Radio City, Times Square and its side streets will be a carnival, churches intermingled, bums sleeping in their doors. No place will remind us of the place we have come from, neither the drab furnished rooms, nor the brightly repainted apartments. Not even the yellow telegram envelopes, my name appearing through the glassine windows, YOUR LETTER MAKE NO PLANS TO STAY THERE LEAVE FOR HOME SATURDAY SURE LETTER FOLLOWS MOTHER, or, later, to seal my assurance, DO NOT SACRIFICE JOB CASH BONUS AND YOUR FAMILY ON ADVICE OF THOSE WITHOUT REAL INTEREST IN YOUR WELFARE AND AGAINST THAT OF ALL WHO HAVE YOUR INTEREST AT HEART STOP YOUR JOB OPEN THIS WEEK NOT AFTERWARD STOP DONT RUIN ALL THREE OF OUR FUTURES SPECIALLY YOURS FRED. There will be daytime sleeping, nighttime waking. There will be strangers, to many of whom I will have nothing to offer, yet with all of whom I will be aware that if I were not empty there might be a rich exchange. There will be a wanderer, bereft of all possessions. But people will not call out "There goes a nothing, a nobody," at him when he passes, but "There goes a character!" There will be joy, riding in stupendous coverings, luring the living into spiritual gates. There will be gadflies. And, waiting always, there will be a pigeonhole for every identity, no matter how known, no matter how small . . .

Wet gray landscape sleeps in the half awake mist beyond the road. A town passes, smelling like a wet gourd. The highway, along which frame houses fade out of sight, is as shining as though it has rained. Then, suddenly, at a stone house with a yard full of geese, the bus curves up an incline onto a low bridge over great flat stretches of the water of Chesapeake Bay. But I am as yet unaware that I have seen my first aware sight of the sea.